The
Elements
of
Mystery
Fiction

Writing the Modern Whodunit

Books by William G. Tapply

Brady Coyne mystery novels:
Death at Charity's Point
The Dutch Blue Error
Follow the Sharks
The Marine Corpse
Dead Meat
The Vulgar Boatman
A Void in Hearts
Dead Winter
Client Privilege
The Spotted Cats
Tight Lines
The Snake Eater
The Seventh Enemy
Close to the Bone
Cutter's Run
Muscle Memory
Scar Tissue
Past Tense
A Fine Line
Shadow of Death

Other novels:
Thicker than Water (with Linda Barlow)
First Light (with Philip R. Craig)

Books on the outdoors:
Those Hours Spent Outdoors
Opening Day and Other Neuroses
Home Water Near and Far
Sportsman's Legacy
A Fly Fishing Life
Bass Bug Fishing
Upland Days
Pocket Water
The Orvis Guide to Fly Fishing for Bass

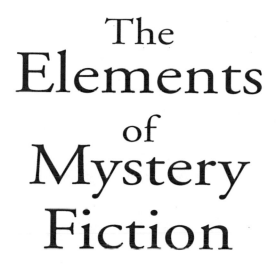

The
Elements
of
Mystery
Fiction

Writing the Modern Whodunit

William G. Tapply

Poisoned Pen Press

Copyright © 1995 by William G. Tapply
Second Edition 2004

10 9 8 7 6 5 4 3 2

Library of Congress Catalog Card Number: © 2004101557

ISBN: 1-59058-115-6 (978-1-59058-115-5)

Poisoned Pen Press
6962 E. First Ave., Ste. 103
Scottsdale, AZ 85251
www.poisonedpenpress.com
info@poisonedpenpress.com

Printed in the United States of America

Acknowledgments

I am indebted to all of the people who have directly and indirectly encouraged me and taught me how to write mystery novels: My editors Betsy Rapoport, Susanne Kirk, Jackie Farber, Otto Penzler, and Keith Kahla; all those who have read and critiqued my crude first efforts, especially Rick Boyer and Vicki Stiefel; my agents, Fred Morris and the late Jed Mattes; and, of course, my role models, all those writers past and present whose stories have entertained and informed me since I learned to read.

Sylvia Burack first encouraged me to write this book and then edited it relentlessly. Barbara Peters is responsible for the appearance of this new edition, and Rob Rosenwald and Jennifer Semon shepherded it through the production process.

Books would not appear on bookshelves without artists, copy editors, production people, publicists, sales reps, and booksellers. I am grateful to all those I've worked with over the years for their good work.

Writers could not persevere without the support of family and friends. I am lucky indeed to have had so many unwavering supporters in my corner: My parents, H. G. and Muriel Tapply; my children, Mike, Melissa, and Sarah Tapply; my stepsons, Ben and Blake Ricciardi; Kate Mattes, who's always been there; my colleagues and my writing students at Clark University; and, especially, my wife and my love, Vicki Stiefel, to whom this book is dedicated.

W.G.T
March 2004

Table of Contents

Introduction
to the Second Edition

A decade ago when I wrote the first edition of this book I worked on an Apple IIe computer. It had no hard drive. The manuscript was printed out on tractor-feed paper in dot matrix and submitted via the United States Postal Service. I saved the text on five-inch floppy disks. It took four of those disks to hold it all.

Today, five computers and ten years later, I am submitting this second edition electronically and saving it on both my hard drive and a CD. All of the additional material that the other contributors wrote came to me attached to emails.

A lot has changed in the world of mystery fiction in the last decade besides the writing technology. Now we have on-line bookstores. Chain super-bookstores have sprung up like mushrooms after a spring rainstorm. We have print-on-demand books and E-books. Tradition-drenched old independent New York publishing houses have become imprints under the umbrellas of giant multinational conglomerates. Small specialty publishers have popped up all over the country to fill the void.

New best-selling authors have burst upon the mystery scene in the past ten years. Several old best-selling authors have passed from the scene.

But some things haven't changed. Good books are still good books, and they're written by solitary, dogged people who know what they're doing and who are willing to hunch over their writing machines for hours every day, through sickness and health, fair weather and foul, month after month to do it.

The elements of mystery fiction and the ways of the successful mystery writer remain constant. Classroom teachers, workshop leaders, and writing tutors who have used *The Elements of Mystery Fiction* with their students have told me not to change a word of it.

They have, however, reported that the first edition fails to address a number of issues that their students repeatedly and predictably raise, issues such as: What are the pros and cons of writing a mystery series versus a standalone thriller? What about collaborating on a novel? Why does everybody insist that an author needs an agent? How do the publishing and book-selling businesses really work? If my novel gets published, how can I help promote it? And the universal question that haunts aspiring mystery writers: Recognizing the odds, do I really have a chance of ever seeing my book in print? Why shouldn't I give up this quixotic dream and take up cabinet making, or gardening, or rock climbing?

To address these valid and important issues, I invited, begged and bribed some of the most prominent and successful people in the mystery business to share their experience and expertise for this new edition.

Philip R. Craig (Chapter 12: "Writing the Mystery Series") is the creator of the long-running Martha's Vineyard mystery series featuring ex-cop, surf fisherman, gourmet cook, and all-round good guy J. W. Jackson. Phil's books have been touted on the television show "Good Morning America."

Bill Eidson (Chapter 13: "Standalone or Series Mystery?") has published six "standalone" novels, three of which have been optioned for movies. Bill's most recent novel, *The Repo*, is the first in a new mystery series.

Hallie Ephron (Chapter 14: "Seeing Double: Making Collaboration Work") is half of the G. H. Ephron team that has collaborated on four (and counting) popular and critically acclaimed mystery novels featuring psychiatrist Dr. Peter Zak.

Fred Morris (Chapter 15: "Doing Business with Agents")

is a veteran literary agent with the Jed Mattes Agency in New York City, which specializes in mystery novels. Fred has worked with both first-time novelists and old-timers.

Barbara Peters (Chapter 16: "Editing and Publishing Mysteries") is the founder, editor-in-chief, and publisher of the Poisoned Pen Press in Scottsdale, Arizona; the proprietor of the Poisoned Pen bookstore; and the editor of several anthologies on mystery writing. Barbara has won a number of awards and is one of the most influential people in the mystery world.

Otto Penzler (Chapter 17: "The Bookselling Business"), owner and proprietor of the Mysterious Bookshop in New York City, has been in the bookselling business for twenty years. He's a publisher and a writer and the editor of numerous mystery short-story anthologies. Otto has won just about every honor the mystery community bestows.

Jeremiah Healy (Chapter 18: "Catch 23: Publicizing Your Mystery Novel") is the creator of both the John Francis Cuddy private-investigator series and (under the pseudonym "Terry Devane") the Mairead O'Clare legal-thriller series. Jerry has written seventeen novels and more than sixty short stories, fourteen of which have won or been nominated for the Shamus Award. He belongs to all of the mystery organizations and has been the keynote speaker at countless conventions.

Vicki Stiefel (Chapter 19: "Persistence") is an expert on her subject. A successful film critic and magazine editor, Vicki served a twelve-year apprenticeship writing, revising, rewriting, and submitting mystery novels before her persistence finally paid off and *Body Parts* was accepted for publication.

I respect and admire all of the contributors to this edition. I am happy and honored to know them as friends as well as colleagues. In fact, Vicki, to whom this book was (and still is) dedicated, is my wife. Her persistence is one of her most lovable traits.

William G. Tapply
Hancock, New Hampshire
September 2003

Introduction

When I began writing my first mystery novel, I thought I had a crackerjack idea. I had invented characters who intrigued me, I had thought up dramatic scenes and tense conflicts, and I had in mind some vivid settings. I knew where my story would start, I could foresee the direction it would take, and I knew how it would end. I had done enough nonfiction writing to feel confident that I could string the words together. I had even sold a few articles.

I had never tried writing mystery fiction. I had never tried to analyze its elements. So what? Writing is writing, I figured.

That first mystery of mine had everything required of a novel—characters and settings and scenes, themes and plots and subplots, dialogue and description and narrative. When it was finished, it made a gratifyingly tall stack of pages. I was rather proud of my accomplishment. I wasn't ready to say I'd written a book, but I had written a book-length manuscript.

It now resides in a cardboard box in the attic, where I lovingly entombed it when I realized that it wasn't very good.

Strangely, I was encouraged by having written a bad novel.

Maybe it's not so strange. The writers I know seem constitutionally unable to allow themselves to be discouraged by failure. Certainly if I had been discouraged, I wouldn't have launched boldly into my second mystery novel. And if I hadn't done that, it never would have been published.

When I started trying to write mystery fiction, I didn't know what I was doing. I'd taken no courses, read no how-to books, belonged to no critique groups.

What I did have were the echoes of hundreds of wonderful books in my head, the deceptively straightforward prose of Dashiell Hammett and Raymond Chandler and Ross Macdonald and the confident narration of Travis McGee and Dr. Watson and Archie Goodwin, and many, many others.

Reading good mysteries taught me everything I knew when I began trying to write them. "Read, read, read," said William Faulkner. "Read everything—trash, classics, good and bad, and see how they do it. Just like a carpenter who works as an apprentice and studies the master. Read! You'll absorb it. Then write. If it is good, you'll find out. If it's not, throw it out the window."

I wrote and published several mystery novels without consciously examining the process or analyzing its elements. It was a profound handicap. Instinct often told me when something wasn't right. But ignorance prevented me from figuring it out and fixing it. My editor made me do a lot of revising and rewriting, but even with her guidance, it often felt like trial and error.

Sometimes groups invited me to talk with them about writing. They asked me difficult questions, such as, "Where do you get your ideas?" and "How do you construct your plots?" and "How do you write realistic dialogue?" and "How do you plant clues fairly without being obvious?" They forced me to think about what I was doing.

At first, I stumbled through my answers. But I studied and analyzed the work of other mystery writers and took every opportunity to discuss the craft with them. I read how-to books and magazine articles. And I gradually began to understand the elements of mystery fiction.

This book is my attempt to isolate and analyze those elements, to identify the variables that make the difference between success and failure, and to help you write publishable mystery fiction.

Part 1

Writing a Modern Whodunit

Chapter 1

The Elements of Mystery Fiction

Mystery fiction was born in 1841 when *Graham's Magazine* published Edgar Allan Poe's short story "The Murders in the Rue Morgue." Here Poe introduces C. Auguste Dupin, the detective who, through his superior intellect and brilliant powers of observation and deduction, sorts out the clues and identifies the murderer of an old woman and her daughter.

The mystery is a puzzler. Dupin is a genius. When he reveals the culprit, readers gasp in admiration.

Literary murders are as old as the book of Genesis. But no one before Poe, as far as we know, ever wrote a story in which the central plot question was "Who did it?" and the hero was a detective who correctly deduced the answer to that question.

If Poe invented mystery fiction, fifty years later Sir Arthur Conan Doyle made it wildly popular. Sherlock Holmes, like Poe's Dupin, is a brilliant detective who gathers clues, ponders them privately, and then fingers the villain in a dramatic scene of revelation near the end of the story. His worshipful roommate and chronicler, Dr. Watson, follows along to report on his friend's activities. Watson is Everyman. He's you, or I, or any reader of average intelligence. Unlike Holmes or his literary predecessor Dupin, Watson is accessible. He speaks directly to readers, who identify with the kindly doctor. He's as baffled by Holmes as readers are, as awed by the detective's deductive powers, as intrigued by his eccentricities.

Conan Doyle, with his down-to-earth narrator, his eccentric genius detective, his sharp portraits of nineteenth-century London, and his mind-bending puzzles, transformed mystery fiction into the stuff of best-sellers, which it has remained ever since.

In the stories of Poe and Doyle and their imitators, mystery readers were not allowed into the minds of literary detectives. Readers had no choice but to remain puzzled while Dupin and Holmes gathered clues and pondered them in private. The reader's reward came when the detective dramatically identified the culprit, explained the villain's method and motive, and enumerated the clues that had led him to his uncanny conclusion.

Agatha Christie converted the mystery into a participatory activity for the reader. Christie introduced the vital and revolutionary element of fair play to mystery fiction, making all the clues that were available to her detective equally available to the reader. Readers who could only watch and marvel at Holmes were invited to look for clues and interpret the behavior of Christie's characters. Readers could match wits with Hercule Poirot or Miss Marple, and when a Christie detective pointed the finger at a murderer, readers could slap their foreheads and say, "Of course! I should have figured that out for myself."

With Christie, mystery reading became a game between writer and reader. "Fool me if you can," begged the reader, "and I'll be disappointed if you don't. I want you to make me admire how cleverly you craft your plot and how well you camouflage your clues. But you'd better play fair."

After Christie, successful mystery yarns did just that. The plots were complex, the puzzles bewildering, the motives obscure, and the murder methods bizarre. The story didn't have to be realistic, nor did the characters need to resemble actual flesh-and-blood people, as long as the clues were laid out fairly—no matter how cleverly they were disguised. The writers of the 1920s and '30s—Dorothy L. Sayers, S. S. Van Dine, Ellery Queen, Erle Stanley Gardner, Rex Stout, and many others—gave readers what they wanted. The period was known as "The Classical Age" of mystery fiction.

Then Dashiell Hammett and Raymond Chandler created their sleuths, Sam Spade and Philip Marlowe. These two American writers introduced mystery readers to the "mean streets" and the flesh-and-blood people who inhabited them. They created the "hard-boiled" mystery, in which gritty settings, three-dimensional characters, true-to-life dialogue, irony, mood, style, and pace were grafted onto the classical detective puzzle.

In other words, Chandler and Hammett gave us novels, mysteries that qualified as genuine works of literature, not merely clever puzzles.

Today's mystery shelves are packed with a rich variety of novels. Contemporary mysteries come in all sizes, styles, themes, and moods—the classic private-eye puzzles of Sue Grafton and Robert B. Parker, the dark brooding novels of James Lee Burke and Lawrence Block, the medical mysteries of Patricia D. Cornwell and Michael Palmer, the police procedurals of Ed McBain and William J. Caunitz, the small-town domestic tales of Katherine Hall Page and Charlotte MacLeod.

But regardless of their genres and sub-genres, contemporary mysteries all contain the same elements:

1. *The puzzle.* The important question that drives the plot of every mystery novel and short story is: Who did it? Who committed the crime (generally murder)? At the beginning, neither the reader nor the story's protagonist knows the answer.

2. *Detection.* The investigation of the crime constitutes the story's central action. When the puzzle is solved, the story ends.

3. *The sleuth as hero.* The protagonist is the character who solves the puzzle, generally through his intelligence, perseverance, courage, physical strength, moral conviction, or a combination of these qualities.

4. *The worthy villain.* The antagonist, generally the murderer, tests the limits of the sleuth's abilities. The villain is clever, resourceful, and single-mindedly intent on getting away with his crime. He makes the puzzle a supreme challenge for both the sleuth and the reader.

5. *Fair play*. All of the evidence uncovered by the sleuth, in the form of clues, is equally available to the reader. The climactic revelation presents no evidence that hasn't already been disclosed in the course of the story.

6. *Realism and logic*. Everything fits, makes sense, and could happen the way it's depicted in the story. Mystery stories take place in actual places, or fictional places that seem real. They are populated with characters who resemble real people. Readers care about these characters, engage them emotionally, and feel as if they know them.

In the years since Hammett and Chandler, thousands of literary murders have been solved by hundreds of sleuths in every corner of the globe. There are so many different styles and approaches to the contemporary mystery that terms such as "police procedural," "private eye," "hard-boiled," "soft-boiled," and "cozy," just to name the most obvious, have evolved to help classify them. There are series and non-series mysteries. They take place in the present, in historical eras, even in the future. They are wry and witty, dark and violent, philosophical and urbane.

Fictional detectives range from professionals (police officers, private investigators, lawyers, district attorneys, forensic patholo-gists, newspaper reporters—those who get paid specifically to investigate murders) to schoolteachers, housewives, teenagers, and other amateurs. They can be female or male, gay or straight, old or young, rich or poor. They work in big cities, suburbs, rural areas, and the wilderness in every state and virtually every nation in the world.

Mystery novels by Tony Hillerman, Sue Grafton, Dick Fran-cis, Barbara Michaels, Robert Parker, Patricia Cornwell, and many others regularly appear on the best-seller lists. Hundreds of other talented writers produce a popular mystery novel every year or two. Many critics contend that some of the very best novel and short-story writers in America and England these days are those who produce mystery fiction.

Every year dozens of "first mysteries" are published. Periodicals such as *Ellery Queen's Mystery Magazine* and *Alfred Hitchcock*

Mystery Magazine are devoted exclusively to short mystery fiction. Editors and publishers continually search for the next popular writer, the next blockbuster mystery novel.

The basic elements of mystery fiction remain constant.

Mystery variants

If the story's driving question is not "Who did it?," and if detection is not the central action of the story, it is not, technically, a mystery. Today's best-seller lists are often top-heavy with high-suspense titles in which the plot's momentum comes from different questions, typically: "Will the bad guy succeed in carrying out his sinister plan before the good guy can stop him?" John Grisham, Mary Higgins Clark, and Tom Clancy, among many others, have made these "thrillers" enormously popular. Crime and justice are central issues in these novels. Since clues, detection, and puzzle-solving frequently play important, if secondary parts of their plots, many of the principles of mystery fiction apply equally to them.

The reader as participant

Contemporary mystery fiction invites readers to join the sleuth in the quest to solve a compelling puzzle. Modern readers will not settle for the role of spectator. They want to participate in your story.

Give your readers credit. Assume they are as smart as you are. "No one can write decently," said E. B. White, "who is distrustful of the reader's intelligence, or whose attitude is patronizing."

The most important advice I can give you is this: *Always think of your audience. Write for your readers. Never deprive them of the chance to participate.*

As we have seen, modern readers expect fair play. You cannot withhold vital clues from them. Everything of consequence that your sleuth encounters must also be encountered by your readers. Unless readers have the evidence, they cannot fairly participate in the solving of the puzzle.

On the other hand, readers don't want to be guided through the puzzle's solution. They want only a fair chance to solve it *for themselves*. They don't want to be given more information than the sleuth has. That would give them an advantage over him, which also violates the rule of fair play. Readers resent having clues explained to them by an all-knowing author as much as they resent having clues withheld from them.

Invite them to walk beside your hero or heroine, seeing, hearing, smelling, tasting and feeling along with your sleuth. No more, no less.

Showing without telling

For mystery writers, the golden rule is: *Show, don't tell.* Give your readers the same kinds of sensory impressions they use in their own lives to interpret their world. Then let them draw their own conclusions. When you explain or elaborate for your readers, you deprive them of the opportunity to participate.

Let your readers encounter your story's characters and situations as they experience their actual lives. When you meet and interact with other people, you *observe* their behavior and then you *interpret* it. People's actions and words are clues to their inner feelings, attitudes, philosophies, and motives. You draw conclusions about others based on the clues they present to you. If you see a man crying, you might conclude that he is sad, or frustrated, or angry, or even happy. You take into account the context of his behavior and everything else you know about him—including the possibility that he might lie to you. Then you make your interpretation. You have no all-knowing narrator to tell you, "He is crying tears of joy" or "He is depressed because he killed his friend."

If a woman slams her fist on a tabletop or curses loudly or clenches her teeth, you might conclude that she's angry. You might be wrong. In fact, she might be trying to make you *believe* she's angry when, in fact, she is trying to manipulate your emotions or make you believe something that isn't true. You can't be sure. You have to consider the clues—the observed behavior and everything else you know about that person—to arrive at your best interpretation. In actual life, no narrator stands at your shoulder whispering in your ear, "That person is angry" or "She's only pretending to be angry."

Just as you *show* your readers the characters in your stories, so should you create settings for them. *Show* your readers a restaurant with a jukebox playing a Patti Page tune, candles in Chianti bottles, and red-and-white-checked oilcloth table-cloths, then allow them to draw their own conclusions about the place. Do not *tell* them, "The restaurant had an old-fashioned '50s atmosphere." Readers can—and want to—deduce that for themselves.

Words such as "sad," "manipulative," and "old-fashioned" tell readers more than they want to know. Let them draw their own conclusions, the way they do in real life. Otherwise you'll turn your readers into passive spectators—and turn them off.

Make your story a series of experiences for your readers. Give them sensory impressions. *Show* them some significant details of people and places, but resist the impulse to tell them what those details mean. Write scenes in which characters act and interact, and put your readers in the middle of those scenes. Allow them to participate, to interpret, to draw conclusions, and to fill in the blanks. Trust them to think for themselves. Respect their intelligence.

Showing without telling gives contemporary readers what they want from a mystery story—a fair chance to participate in the puzzle's solution.

Chapter 2

Finding Your Story

The question writers are most often asked by non-writers is: "Where do you get your ideas?"

Typically, writers reply, "Why, ideas are everywhere. The newspapers. Television. Cocktail party conversation. Dreams. The problem isn't finding ideas. The problem is recognizing those that can be converted into a story, and then knowing how to create that story."

Sometimes they just smile and say, "Serendipity."

The most honest answer to the question is: "Ideas come from inside my head. If you want a story idea, that's where you have to look."

Sure, there are plenty of ideas. But the workable idea, the one that will sustain a compelling mystery plot, is rare and precious. To recognize a good idea and develop it into a story requires a lot of hard, critical thought and planning.

Sometimes writers are fired by the inspiration of what strikes them as a good idea and are so eager to begin writing that they don't stop to think. They rush to their keyboards and begin writing. They expect their idea to sustain them. They are devastated when, after a few pages or a few chapters, they run out of steam. Their idea did not sustain them, because they failed to nurture and develop it into a fully imagined story.

Planning your story requires more than the inspiration of a good idea. The creative process that precedes actual writing is unique to each writer. Here's how I do it:

Brady Coyne, the lawyer-sleuth hero of my mystery series, likes to ponder difficult cases from the banks of a trout stream or the little balcony off his waterfront apartment in Boston. The process is identical to what I, his creator, go through trying to think up puzzles for him to solve:

> I drank and smoked and thought. The breeze came at me from the sea, moist and organic. The bell buoy out there clanged its mournful rhythm. From behind me came the muffled city noises—the wheeze of traffic through the night-time streets, the occasional punctuation of siren and horn, the almost subsonic hum and murmur of dense human life.
>
> I remembered the Vermont woods, and my picnic with Kat, and how the birds and bugs and animals and river sounded, and how the pine forest smelled, and how my rainbow trout never missed his mayfly.
>
> And while one part of my mind registered all of these surface things and wandered freely on its own associations, a different part of it looked for pattern and purpose in three North Shore murders, and a third part watched what was going on and tried not to judge it or guide it.

That, as well as I can state it, is how I think through a story idea. It's a process of disciplined free association, at once random and purposeful. If anyone watched me do it, they'd accuse me of daydreaming.

I do it on long automobile trips. I tend to miss highway exits when I'm driving. During conversations, I find myself saying, "Excuse me. What were you saying?" Sometimes I lie on my bed and stare at the insides of my eyelids. Now and then I scribble a note about a character or a place or an event on a scrap of paper. Periodically I enter my notes into my computer. I build scenes around them and explore them and try to see where they lead.

More often than not they take me to a dead end. I expect that and keep at it. A good idea is worth working for.

An idea isn't a plot, and a plot isn't a story. An idea is a spark that ignites the individual creative imagination. It can usually be stated in a simple declarative statement, such as, "An elderly woman dying of cancer yearns to reconcile with her estranged daughter before she dies."

Or, "The owner of a million-dollar stamp, thought to be the only one of its kind in existence, is contacted by someone who claims to possess a duplicate of that stamp."

You may not find either of these ideas particularly promising. But I did, and I developed each of them into a novel. An idea that excites me may not strike your imagination, for the obvious reason that you and I have different interests and experiences.

An idea sets off a complicated chain reaction, a sequence of imagined events which the writer converts into scenes populated by imaginary people. That is a plot. When the writer puts it all onto paper, it becomes a story.

In their search for ideas, some mystery writers hang around with newspaper reporters, or sit in courtrooms, or lurk in barrooms, or ride with police officers. I know one writer who tunes in the afternoon television talk shows. He claims he's gotten several story ideas from the oddball people interviewed by Oprah and Jerry Springer.

Always be alert for ideas. Read compulsively and eclectically. Eavesdrop shamelessly. Visit new places. Study people. Engage strangers in conversation. And when you get an idea that excites you, resist the powerful temptation to sit down immediately and start writing. Instead, find a quiet place where you can practice the discipline of controlled free association.

The best way to create a complex mystery plot from a single exciting idea is to keep asking yourself: "What if?" Here's an example of how this works for me:

The idea for my first novel, *Death at Charity's Point*, came from the news story of a fugitive from the law who, after several years of living quietly under an assumed identity, a pillar of his little rural community, decided to turn himself in.

What if, I asked myself, someone in this fugitive's little community had uncovered his true identity? And *what if* he didn't want to be brought to justice? *What if* he committed murder to protect his secret?

This struck me as a promising idea for a mystery novel. I stated it for myself in the form of a premise: "A former '60s radical, wanted by the FBI and living under an assumed identity, commits murder to protect her secret." I then bombarded the premise with more what-if questions. *What if* the murder appeared to be a suicide? *What if* the victim's elderly mother refused to believe her son would take his own life? *What if* she engaged the family lawyer to investigate? *What if* the murderer committed more murders? *What if* she targeted the lawyer for death?

Asking those "what if" questions often felt random and unproductive. For every useful answer, dozens led nowhere. But I kept asking them until I believed I had a coherent story. Then I created and revised outlines, wrote character sketches, and explored possible settings.

The source of my idea had been televised nationally. But as far as I know, no one else used it as the basis for a mystery novel. It worked for me because it merged with that unique entity that is my imagination, which is the product of my peculiar history, personality, and life experiences.

And if it had happened to inspire someone else, their novel would without doubt have been unrecognizably different from mine.

The formula that generally works for me is: CHARACTER + PROBLEM = STORY IDEA. The character is usually either a murderer or the victim of a murderer. That character's story becomes the basis for the novel. But it's not the novel itself.

The two stories of the mystery

Mystery fiction, remember, tells a tale of detection. It's a puzzle. It raises the "whodunit" question and sets the sleuth off on her quest. Along the way she encounters clues until she—and the reader—have learned enough to solve the puzzle.

Before you write this story of detection, *you must first write the story of the murder itself.* It's a chronological tale. It begins with the relationship between the victim and the murderer, explains the murderer's motive, and develops through the planning and execution of the deed.

What clues will you scatter along the way? What other innocent characters are associated with the victim? Might they, too, have motive, means, and opportunity to commit murder? How has the culprit covered his tracks? What are the relationships among all of these characters? Where does the story take place? How do elements in the setting contribute to the story's events?

Answering all of these questions will give you a story of murder.

Write a narrative sketch of this straightforward tale. Tell it chronologically. Populate it with husbands and wives, lovers and ex-spouses, business acquaintances and estranged friends. Compose the life story of your victim. Be sure he has plenty of potential enemies. Then do the same for your murderer.

This sketch could itself be the plot for a novel. With fascinating multidimensional characters, complex relationships, a powerful underlying moral question, a touch of irony, and intense conflicts, it might even make a very good suspense novel or thriller.

But because this is the story of the villain and his victim, it's not yet a mystery. The mystery story belongs to the sleuth.

To create a mystery, you must convert the linear murderer-victim story into a puzzle and create a puzzle-solving hero. This is the specific challenge for the mystery writer. You must invent two stories for every one you write. First you must think up the story of the crime. Only then can you write your mystery novel, *which is the story of that crime's detection.*

Book-length mysteries are, in all respects, *novels.* A mystery novel, just like a "literary novel," should be populated with fascinating multidimensional characters. It should ask important moral questions. Mystery fiction, every bit as much as the mainstream variety, can explore the complexity of the human spirit and the irony of the human condition. The best ones do exactly that.

But mystery fiction offers a bonus. The bonus is the puzzle.

Here's how I constructed the two stories that became my eleventh Brady Coyne novel, *Tight Lines*:

I decided to explore the difficult and intense relationships that inevitably develop between psychiatrists and their patients in the course of psychoanalysis. Patients, in some cases, fall in love with and may attempt to seduce their analysts, whose professional ethic requires them to resist powerful temptations while continuing to treat their patients. This doctor-patient relationship was the idea for my story.

Sometimes psychiatrists succumb to temptation. "What if," I thought, "a psychiatrist had an affair with his beautiful female patient?"

And, because my story had to be a mystery, I next asked: "What if that patient were murdered?"

The storyline that resulted went this way: Mary Ellen Ames worshipped her father, who died when she was in college. Mary Ellen cut off ties with her mother and proceeded to engage in a series of love affairs with older men, many of them married. She became involved with drugs and had a homosexual encounter. After several years she decided to seek psychiatric help. She chose Dr. Warren McAllister, a middle-aged psychoanalyst who reminded her of her father, gradually seduced him, and then threatened to expose him to his wife and his professional associates if he didn't agree to marry her.

I thought hard and long about Mary Ellen Ames and Warren McAllister and his wife. I created Mary Ellen's lovers—the married college professor, the bookstore owner who supplied her with drugs, the suspended Boston policeman who lived in a trailer, the troubled young woman who lived in Mary Ellen's apartment building. I gave Mary Ellen's mother a story, too. She lived alone in the Ames family mansion. She was suffering from terminal cancer and wanted to reconcile with her estranged daughter before she died.

From this lineup of characters I selected a murderer.

Then I was ready to write a detailed narrative summary of this story, complete with all of the characters' life histories, personalities, and strongly felt needs and desires. The process took me several weeks of difficult and frustrating trial-and-error thinking.

Only when I felt I knew this story thoroughly did I begin converting it into a mystery novel which, I knew, would be propelled by the puzzle question: Who killed Mary Ellen Ames?

Because I have a series character, my lawyer Brady Coyne had to serve as the puzzle-solver. So the first question I had to answer was: How would Brady get involved with the case?

I decided that Susan Ames would ask Brady, her family lawyer, to track down her daughter. The story of detection was underway.

Then came the puzzle's development, the unfolding of clues, false trails, and red herrings. Brady tries to track down Mary Ellen. He learns where she lives, but she hasn't been home in more than a week. He convinces the building's superintendent to let him into Mary Ellen's apartment, where he finds a bottle of prescription medicine. This leads him to Dr. McAllister, the psychiatrist, who eventually confides in Brady that he's been having an affair with Mary Ellen but insists that he doesn't know where she is.

Eventually, Mary Ellen's body is found in a New Hampshire pond. Based on the medical examiner's report, the police call it an accidental drowning, but Brady has his doubts. By now, he's encountered some of the people in Mary Ellen's life, all of whom could have a motive for murdering the young woman.

As Brady investigates, the stakes grow higher. What began as a search for a missing woman becomes a desperate race against time and a murderer who will kill again. Ultimately, Brady finds himself endangered.

And so forth, to the ultimate revelation.

I wrote a narrative summary of this story of detection, too, taking elements of the first storyline and placing them into the second. I laid out the story's various turning points—the opening scene with the dying mother, Brady's encounters with each of the people in Mary Ellen's life, the discovery of Mary Ellen's body. I converted facts from the first story into clues, dead-end trails, false suspects, and misleading assumptions.

As the story took shape, it transformed itself into a sequence of scenes, each of which moved the story forward, introduced new information, raised new questions, complicated the puzzle, and jacked up the stakes.

When I summarized all of the scenes, I was ready to write the book. I knew my story. I had direction and purpose.

Of course, some things changed. As the characters began to participate in actual scenes, they came to life. I discovered that some of them had depths and contradictions and motivations I hadn't originally imagined, which suggested modifications in the plot. I was receptive to changes, but skeptical, too; I considered them carefully before incorporating them into my story.

In the end, when the solution to the puzzle was revealed, I hoped that readers could say that everything fit together, the clues were fair, and they knew as much as Brady did. They had experienced my story as a participant, not a mere spectator. I also hoped they would then say, "I should have figured it out for myself. But it fooled me."

The case of the short story

The elements of mystery short stories are no different from those of novels. No matter how short, every story has a plot, a setting, and characters. It contains a combination of narrative and dialogue. It has a beginning, a middle, and an end.

To say that a short story is the same as the novel except that it is shorter, however, is to ignore some fundamental differences between the two forms. The short story makes special demands on the writer.

Some of these demands are relatively obvious. The short story involves just a few characters—perhaps only one or two. It typically uses only one setting and a single point of view. It occurs over a short period of time—often as a single event that unfolds without interruption. Descriptions are spare. Characters and settings are drawn with a few deft strokes. Every detail must serve a purpose. Dialogue is spare and to the point.

In other words, nothing is wasted in the short story, which typically runs from 1,500 to 5,000 words—twenty or more times shorter than an average novel. Regardless of the story's length, the writer must strive to make every paragraph, every sentence, every word serve a purpose. Rarely can the short story accommodate extended descriptive passages or flashbacks, rambling dialogue, extraneous secondary characters, or subplots. Short stories can be difficult and time-consuming to write, but they are meant to be read in a single uninterrupted sitting. The short story contains a single, focused narrative purpose.

The "purpose" of the short story is to dramatize just one point, which can usually be stated as the story's theme: Crime doesn't pay (or, crime sometimes *does* pay); a crisis will bring out the best (or the worst) in people; revenge is sweet (or bitter); love conquers all (or hatred conquers love). The story is written with the single-minded aim of dramatizing its point. It teaches a lesson in human nature, it contains a moral, it offers an insight.

The payoff of the mystery short story comes in the form of a surprise or twist at the climax. It gives the reader a "punch." The entire story is written to dramatize the meaning of that climactic revelation.

Anything that does not contribute to maximizing the impact of the punch should be eliminated.

The punch of most mystery short stories dramatizes the simple theme that things are not what they appear to be. In the classical whodunit story, for example, the most likely suspect is innocent (although in the focused, economical short story, the actual villain may not be revealed if that is not the story's point). Other mystery storylines focus on the discovery of an unexpected motive for murder, or the surprising meaning of a single puzzling clue, or the unforeseen relationship between the villain and the victim, or a revealing event in one character's past.

Things are not what they seem. Dramatizing what they actually are is the story's point. It offers the reader a new insight—into human nature, into the ironies of life, into the meaning of love, or hate, or death, or greed. After reading an effective short story, the reader should stop for a moment and think, "Ah, yes. I never thought of it that way before."

The short story contains the same structural elements as the novel:

1. Situation—Virtually all fiction of any length focuses on an interesting character with a problem. A detective is hired to solve a crime. A murderer attempts to escape detection. A husband seeks to find his missing wife. A compulsive gambler seeks to win back everything he's lost. Short-story situations can be less dramatic and highly charged than those that move novels. The situation in a short story is often commonplace, something that the average reader can identify with. But the situation must be important to the story's protagonist, whose goal (to resolve the problem) gives momentum to the story.

2. Complication—The situation creates the story's motivation. It forces the character to act to achieve his or her goal. This action produces more and greater problems. Obstacles arise in the form of a new situation and/or another character (the antagonist) who opposes the protagonist.

3. Climax—The protagonist arrives at the crisis, the turning point in the action, the moment when he or she must make the right decision or fail to achieve his or her goal.

4. Resolution—If the protagonist took the right actions, the problem is solved. If not, the problem remains unresolved, or even more complicated than it was at the beginning, depending on the point the story is making. In any case, the story's resolution must relate directly to the situation it began with, and it must result directly from the actions of the protagonist.

You can achieve interesting short-story effects by altering the natural chronological order in which these structural elements occur. For example, you can begin with the climax (the moment when the protagonist must decide whether to break into his boss's office or walk away) or even the resolution (the protagonist is being pronounced guilty by the jury), then tell the rest of the story as flashback. Or you can use the complication (the protagonist is confronted by the antagonist) as your narrative hook.

Many mystery writers find the short story form, with all of its constraints and demands, more difficult than the novel. They think in terms of novel-length fiction, and when an idea attracts them, they develop and complicate it for the novel form. Others are drawn to the focus and discipline of the short story. Most writers, however, agree that the short-story form forces them to write well, and for this reason alone, even if your goal is to publish a novel, you should try to write short stories.

Chapter 3

The Protagonist: The Sleuth As Hero or Heroine

An editor rejected my first novel with these words: "I think it would take something really unusual to convince us to take on a new mystery series—an Armenian/Jewish plumber who solves cases by listening at people's drain pipes, or something like that."

The point, of course, was this: Publishers—and readers—look for unusual and fascinating protagonists. In fact, in mystery fiction appealing sleuths are at least as important as clever storylines.

A compelling protagonist can sell an ordinary plot. Characters make stories seem real. Readers invest their emotions in characters, not plots. They experience strong feelings—happiness, sadness, anger, worry, fear—because they care about what happens to the characters.

In the case of mystery fiction, the character readers care most about is the sleuth.

A mystery plot is basically the story of the hero or heroine's problems. The most compelling problem, of course, is the puzzle, the "whodunit" question. Mystery storylines are driven by the process of detection. The story belongs to the detective. The sleuth is the one with the problem.

In the mystery, things happen because the protagonist *makes* them happen. Your heroine is the story's catalyst. She is active, not reactive. She doesn't sit around waiting for things to happen to her. She works hard to uncover and interpret clues—they are never given to her gratuitously. She is not passive. She desperately wants to solve the puzzle, and she strives passionately to do it. She has goals and she struggles against powerful obstacles to achieve them. She takes risks, confronts threats, and doesn't quit.

Things are never easy for the heroine or hero.

Make your readers worry about your protagonist and you've got them all the way to The End.

The mystery is a quest story. The sleuth strives to uncover a villain who doesn't want to be uncovered and will do anything—even murder the sleuth—to prevent it. The mystery builds tension and suspense as the sleuth confronts danger in pursuit of the quest.

The sleuth typically has many of the characteristics of the mythical hero—purity of purpose, courage, conviction, and single-minded commitment to ideals. John D. MacDonald's Travis McGee, for example, thinks of himself as a crusader. In *The Dreadful Lemon Sky*, MacDonald writes:

> It is unseemly to feel festive about checking out the death of a dead friend. But there is something heartening about having a sense of mission. A clean purpose. A noble intent, no matter how foolish. ... Ahead, some murky mystery locked in the broken skull of a dead lady. The knight errant, earning his own self-esteem, holding the palms cupped to make a dragon trap.

The stories of most successful mystery writers similarly hinge on their hero or heroine setting off to solve a mystery with a "sense of mission," a "clean purpose," and a "noble intent." Robert Parker's Spenser is clearly a hero from the Travis McGee mold. So, in their own ways, are Sue Grafton's Kinsey Millhone, Sara Paretsky's V. I. Warshawski, Lawrence Block's Matt Scudder, and many others.

Think of your sleuth as a noble—but human and accessible—knight errant. Make your mystery stories journeys—for your hero or heroine, for your readers, and for yourself.

This is the storyline of virtually every successful mystery story: The sleuth has big problems, and as the story unfolds, these problems grow bigger and more baffling and dangerous. But the sleuth perseveres.

Readers convert the sleuth's quest into a question: Will he or she succeed? Make readers care, keep them in doubt, and you'll keep them reading.

Mystery heroes and heroines can be many things—lawyers, hairdressers, children, or Armenian plumbers—but they cannot be weak-willed, passive, or indecisive. Sleuths make things happen. They do not wait for things to happen to them. They succeed because they're aggressive and stubborn—not because they're lucky.

Mystery protagonists, in other words, are not wimps.

Auguste Dupin and Sherlock Holmes weren't wimps, nor were Nero Wolfe or Sam Spade, Philip Marlowe or Travis McGee, Perry Mason or Mike Hammer. Sue Grafton's Kinsey Millhone and Sara Paretsky's V.I. Warshawski aren't wimps. Neither are Tony Hillerman's Jim Chee or Patricia Cornwell's Kay Scarpetta or any of Ed McBain's cops at the 87th Precinct.

Idiosyncratic, yes. Distinctive, definitely. Flawed, human, and accessible. Some heroes and heroines welcome physical confrontations, while others prefer mental contests. But none of them is a wimp.

Study these and other protagonists of successful mystery fiction. I guarantee you'll find them all strong-willed, capable, smart, admirable, persevering, and likeable—the kind of people that readers respect, identify with, and root for. Mystery sleuths know what they're after, they want it badly, and they take risks to achieve it.

This does not mean that heroes and heroines must be bigger than life. If they never fail, or if they're know-it-alls, the outcome of their quest will never be in doubt, and your story will lack tension and suspense. They can—and should—have blind spots, quirks, and weaknesses which they must struggle to overcome.

Their human limitations make them appealing to readers and complicate their quest.

The sleuth you create is as important to the success of your story as the plot.

First you must give him or her a job.

The professional sleuth

The professionals who get paid specifically to solve murders include homicide cops, private investigators, criminal lawyers, prosecuting attorneys, newspaper or television reporters, and forensic pathologists. Their motivation is never in doubt. They investigate murders because that's how they earn a living, and they do it relentlessly and well because they are committed and talented.

The professional sleuth is an otherwise ordinary person whose job happens to involve investigating murders. He may be an overweight recovering alcoholic with an ex-wife who haunts him for alimony and estranged children he never sees and colleagues who refuse to cooperate with him. She may live in a run-down trailer park, be pestered by an amorous vacuum-cleaner sales-man, suffer from menopause, smoke mentholated cigarettes, own an ancient Volkswagen with bad brakes, and live on Diet Coke and Tums.

Professional sleuths persevere regardless of their problems. If they didn't, they wouldn't be effective fictional heroines and heroes.

For one thing, they need the money. That's a good start, but it's not enough. Other powerful motivations such as loyalty, anger, love, or fear drive them.

The higher the stakes for your sleuth—the more he or she stands to gain or lose—the more compelling your story will be, and the faster your reader will turn the pages.

The writer whose sleuth is a professional has a built-in solution to the problem of how to get the story's quest underway. Chapter One opens when an elderly man walks into the office, slumps into a chair, and says: "My wife is missing. I'll pay you to find her. I'll pay you whatever you want."

Or the chief of detectives growls: "Senator Smith's body was found floating in the river last night. He was shot three times in the face. Find out who murdered him, and do it fast. Your promotion depends on it."

Or the editor says: "A bomb exploded in a convenience store. Three people died. Get the story and get it today, or I'll find someone else who will."

Thus do professionals begin their investigation. Their reputations, their self-esteem, their careers, and perhaps their lives are at stake.

Your story has begun.

If you decide your hero or heroine will be a professional, you must be thoroughly familiar with that profession. Don't try to fake it. Every detail must be absolutely accurate. Your cop must think like a cop, talk like a cop, and behave like a cop. Your lawyer must know the law. Your reporter must know how to meet a deadline. Your pathologist must know medicine.

When you write a mystery story, you and your reader make a bargain: Your reader agrees to pretend that your story actually happened, provided you agree to make your story resemble reality. A single misstep or false note will break the contract by shattering your readers' faith—their "willing suspension of disbelief."

The amateur sleuth

An amateur sleuth—a person whose livelihood does not depend on investigating murders—can, at least in theory, come from any walk of life. Housewives and kindergarten teachers, secretaries and bartenders, jockeys and tennis players, computer nerds and real estate brokers—all can find themselves in situations where they might need to solve a murder. A husband might be driven to find his wife's killer, for example, and readers will readily believe that a parent would stop at nothing to track down the kidnapper of a child.

The challenge for the writer is to give amateur sleuths powerfully compelling reasons to pursue their own investigations instead of hiring a professional.

They must be strongly driven to persevere, even when the stakes get higher and the risks multiply. If readers don't buy the amateur sleuth's motive, the story, no matter how clever and dramatic it might otherwise be, will flop.

The motive should result from the story's events, not your sleuth's personality. It's not enough to portray your hero or heroine as naturally curious or brave or persistent. You must create a situation that compels even the most reluctant protagonist to take action.

Since amateurs bring no necessary experience or expertise to the murder investigation, the writer who decides on an amateur can usually avoid the intense research that goes into creating a believable professional.

If you give your amateur hero a convincing reason to chase down a murderer no matter what the danger, a reason that readers can empathize with, you'll sink your hook in deep.

The amateur is likely to change more than the professional as she pursues her investigation. The amateur has probably never before been particularly courageous or resourceful or persevering, and certainly has never had to track down a killer. Now she is forced into a situation that tests her will and courage and intelligence as they have never been tested before.

Gender, appearance, and other characteristics

Your sleuth can be old or young, rich or poor, gay or straight, lighthearted or gloomy, strong or weak, attractive or plain. There are no formulas and no taboos.

James Lee Burke's Dave Robicheaux is a recovering alcoholic. Barbara Neely's Blanche White is an African-American housekeeper. Lawrence Block's Bernie Rhodenbarr is a burglar who runs a bookstore. Jake Page's Mo Bowdre is a blind sculptor. Dana Stabenow's Kate Shugak is an Alaskan Aleut detective.

Tony Hillerman's Jim Chee and Joe Leaphorn are Navajo policemen. Linda Barnes' Carlotta Carlyle plays volleyball and drives a cab. Robert Parker's Spenser is a weightlifter and a gourmet cook. Katherine Hall Page's Faith Fairchild is the wife of a minister and a former New York caterer. All are popular and memorable sleuths.

Mix and match gender, job, hobby, personal history, appearance, and other characteristics to create your own unique, complex, multidimensional sleuth.

The series sleuth

The recurring hero or heroine is a staple of mystery fiction. When considering a first novel for publication, acquiring editors often base their decision on the promise of future novels with the same sleuth. They know that readers develop strong loyalties to appealing heroines and heroes. Mystery readers often care as much about the sleuth's personal problems as they do about the puzzle she's working on.

But the series sleuth must be designed for the long haul. If your first novel features a librarian as a protagonist, you'd better be able to convince an editor that your librarian is an internationally renowned expert in rare and valuable books who is periodically called upon to consult in cases of theft and forgery.

A psychologist whose specialty is child abuse, such as Jonathan Kellerman's Alexander Delaware, makes an effective series hero. So does Rick Boyer's Doc Adams, a forensic dentist. An auto mechanic who's an expert at identifying stolen vehicles could be a series hero. So could a professor of sociology who wrote her doctoral dissertation on rape, or a museum curator or an antique collector whose expertise makes him a useful adviser to those who investigate crimes for a living. But unless you give your series sleuth an area of specialization that could logically involve her in mystery puzzles, you will be hard-pressed to think up an entire series of cases for her.

If you intend to write a series, then make your sleuth either a professional (private investigator, police officer, crime reporter, lawyer) or an amateur with special crime-busting credentials.

But you have to sell your first book before you need to begin worrying about a series. If you've dreamed up a can't-miss storyline that demands an amateur one-shot hero, that's the book you should write. Elmore Leonard and Dick Francis and many other successful mystery authors create new heroes for every story. They thereby avoid the trap that ensnared Conan Doyle, who became so bored with Sherlock Holmes that he killed him off. Eventually Doyle was forced to revive his famous detective when readers made it clear that they wanted only Holmes stories from him.

Defining characters by what they want

Your sleuth should obviously be drawn with the greatest care. You want your readers to identify with her, root for her, agonize with her when she fails, exult with her when she triumphs. Make them care about her happiness and her health and her success. Make them wonder how she's getting along with her ex-husband or lover. Make them hope she'll have a chance to take a vacation, or play more tennis, or visit her father in the nursing home. You want readers to wish your sleuth would eat more sensibly and quit smoking and finally settle down with that elusive young policeman.

Making readers bring these concerns to your books doesn't happen by accident. In the process of developing mystery heroes and heroines, you must explore their full range of interests, desires, needs, and fears.

Everything that goes into characterizing your sleuth can be expressed in terms of what she wants. Readers will worry about her because she has goals that are important to her and it's not certain that she'll achieve them.

Every mystery hero or heroine, like every real person, has several needs and desires. These goals may conflict with each other and with those of other characters. Such conflicts lend depth and texture to your story. Your sleuth, for example, may want to follow the trail of a killer from Chicago to Baltimore. But he also wants his wife to be happy, and she doesn't want him to leave her home alone to watch over their wayward teen-aged son (who wants to skip school and experiment with marijuana).

But your readers will not be satisfied with a novel about your sleuth unless a whodunit puzzle is its focus. In every novel, no matter what other problems your heroine has to confront, she wants above all to solve a crime.

This purpose supersedes all of her other goals. If it didn't, she'd go visit her father or play tennis instead of tracking down the bad guy.

Define your story by your sleuth's motivation. What does she want? Why does she want it so badly? Why does she care enough to take significant risks to attain it?

Then identify your villain's goals, and make sure that his wants are strongly felt and in direct conflict with your sleuth's.

Mystery novels focus on the needs and goals of their characters: The sleuth wants to unravel the clues, identify the villain, and bring him to justice; the villain wants to elude the hero, escape detection, and get away with murder. Many of your characters' goals will not be readily apparent to your readers. Those that are hidden help to create the story's mystery. Deducing the true aims of the villain, for example, typically forms a vital part of the story of detection.

For each important goal, decide why the character needs or wants it so much. Then create scenes that suggest those goals. Your characters' actions are clues to their goals.

A mystery plot can be understood as an evenly matched game between protagonist and antagonist. The stakes are high. Both have important goals and want desperately to achieve them. But it's a zero-sum game. If the hero or heroine wins, the villain must lose.

Creating character profiles

Write down everything you can think of about your characters. Your hero or heroine, your villain, and your other central characters deserve fully developed biographies. Include family histories, birthplaces, schooling, marriages, personal triumphs and tragedies. Think of what your characters like to read and eat and the music they enjoy. What are their politics and their opinions on current issues? How do they like to spend their leisure time? What do they worry about? What do they believe in?

Visualize them. How old are they? What do they look like? What kinds of clothes do they wear?

Imagine their surroundings, too. Draw a word sketch of their house or apartment and their office. Is it neat or cluttered? What paintings hang on the walls? What magazines are on the coffee table?

All of this creative work is background, the writer's necessary homework. You must know your characters fully before you write about them. But be prepared to leave much of this biographical material out of your story.

After creating a dramatic opening scene in which a corpse is discovered and your sleuth appears, you might be tempted to interrupt your story to tell your readers all about your hero:

> He peered into the mirror, scraping his razor carefully around the raised red scar that ran from the corner of his mouth to his jaw, and he remembered that fateful night in New Orleans when Millie O'Leary, the blonde in the black velvet dress, with the glass eye...

And if you're not careful, you'll allow your character to remember all of the delightful material from that biography you worked so hard to create. From the night in New Orleans, you'll recount your hero's childhood, and how the playground bully always stole his lunch money, and how his father said that if he ever wanted to be a man he'd have to learn to stand up to bullies and defend himself. His mother hated violence, and Mom and Dad had big arguments about it. Your hero knew that it was his fault that his parents fought all the time, so he secretly joined a gym and met an ex-prizefighter, who…

And so on and on and on. By now your readers have completely lost track of your story and are likely to set your book aside.

Don't allow the biographies you've composed to limit your imagination and creativity. If, once your story is underway, you find that your characters begin saying and doing unexpected things, don't resist them. Characters often do "come alive" in the story as they never do in sketches and biographies.

Characterization through scenes

In real life, the more we listen to people talk and watch them act, the more we know about them. The same is true in fiction.

Mystery readers prefer to learn about fictional characters the way they get to know real people: by watching them and listening to them.

Everything characters say or do is a clue to their personalities, their life histories, and the forces that motivate them. As they act and speak in scenes, your characters will gradually acquire depth and complexity. Good writers reveal what their characters are like by showing them in action.

In a mystery story, of course, things are never what they appear to be. For example, suppose your readers first meet a character named Harry when he enters a tavern. He straddles a stool, nods to the bartender, and says, "Gimme a Bud."

A moment later Mr. Rowan appears. He slides onto the adjacent barstool, adjusts the crease in his pants, and says, "Excuse me, bartender, but what do you have by way of German beers?"

In this simple scene readers will find clues to the education, experience, taste, appearance, and attitudes of two characters. Readers will expect conflict between these two, and as the scene develops they will learn more about them.

As you show Harry and Mr. Rowan interacting with other characters in this and in later scenes, readers may gradually deduce that the crude Harry, in fact, is a philosophy professor, while the well-dressed and cosmopolitan Mr. Rowan is a Mafia hit man. That process of discovery and surprise is what makes mystery stories compelling for readers.

Chapter 4

The Lineup: Villains, Victims, Suspects, and Other Characters

In mystery fiction, although several characters might have valid motives for committing a murder, only the villain did it. He kills for compelling—but rarely obvious—reasons, and then uses his considerable intelligence to avoid being detected. He presents a supreme challenge to the detective. He makes no mistakes. He never panics. He leaves no blatant clues behind. He never acts guilty. He lies convincingly. He misdirects anyone who might begin to suspect him. He'll do anything—including committing more murders—to avoid being nabbed.

It's even money he'll get away with it. It will take a clever, resourceful, and determined sleuth—and reader—to identify him and bring him to justice. When you write mystery fiction, if you make it easy, you make it boring.

Readers should meet the villain early in the story. At this point, of course, only the writer knows who the villain is and what he or she has done, or is about to do. For the mystery writer, the rule is this: Make the villain one of the crowd, neither more nor less prominent than any of the story's other characters.

Only with the climactic revelation do you transform the villain from an ordinary character into one of great complexity. After all, who'd have suspected that she was capable of all those murders?

Beginning writers tend to worry that unless their villain acts guilty, or appears evil, or has a transparent motive, or is obviously stronger or craftier or more unscrupulous than the other characters, they are not playing fair with their readers. Resist the temptation to throw in clues for your readers' benefit while withholding them from your heroine or hero. And never allow your sleuth to miss a clue that is obvious to your reader. That's giving the reader an unfair advantage—and mystery readers don't want an advantage over the sleuth.

If your readers lose respect for your sleuth, you'll lose your readers.

A worthy villain challenges your hero or heroine and leaves the story's outcome in doubt. Match a determined sleuth against a resourceful and clever and equally determined villain and you'll have your readers hooked.

Suspects and red herrings

In the course of pursuing her investigation, your sleuth encounters a variety of characters who are linked to the victim and could have had the means, motive, and opportunity to commit the murder. The more legitimate suspects your story has, and the longer you keep them under suspicion, the more complicated and challenging your puzzle will be.

Don't disappoint your readers by exonerating too many suspects too quickly. Remember: Only one is the actual villain. All the rest are "red herrings," characters who, despite appearances, are innocent and whose main function in the story is to misdirect the reader's attention. But don't introduce red herrings for the sole purpose of misleading your readers. Every character should have a crucial part to play in the story, offering information of some kind that either helps your sleuth gather clues or misdirects her (and your readers). All characters, however minor, must have motives and goals that connect to the victim and the events of the story.

You can test the validity of a suspect by asking this question: If I omitted this character entirely, would my story collapse?

Your answer must be "yes." Otherwise you're not playing fair.

Victims

In some stories, a character's simple function is to trigger the mystery by getting murdered. The sleuth may begin by investigating this murder, but soon more complicated questions arise, and the victim turns out to be a minor character whose significance fades as the story develops.

More often, however, a murder victim has secrets that provide the murderer with a motive. The connection between the victim's secret and the murderer's motive is the solution to the puzzle.

Mystery fiction typically begins with the discovery of a corpse. The victim is already dead, and readers never get to know him directly. Even in stories where the murder occurs after readers have met the victim, they don't know everything about him. An important part of the sleuth's investigation becomes the painstaking piecing together of the victim's backstory, which comes in bits and pieces of information, often seemingly contradictory, filtered through the memories and motives and lies of other characters.

Who was this person? What did he do and know? Who'd want to kill him?

You must know the answers to these questions before you begin writing. Next to your hero or heroine, your victims—even if readers first meet them as dead bodies—are often the most important and interesting characters in mystery fiction.

Write the life story of your victim before you begin to write your story of detection. Make it rich and complicated and unusual. Give him or her friends and lovers, opponents and enemies. Above all, give him secrets.

Remember, something absolutely fascinating happened to this character: He got murdered.

Sidekicks, lovers, and friends

Holmes has Watson, Nero Wolfe has Archie, Travis McGee has Meyer, Spenser has Hawk. Every mystery sleuth, like every real-life person, has relatives and lovers, casual acquaintances and best friends, adversaries and enemies. These secondary characters make your sleuth's life full and complex and interesting. Most of them serve several functions at once.

Mystery heroes cannot be in more than one place at a time. They also need sounding boards, trusted friends in whom they can confide, allies who can offer them insights and interpretations, raise doubts, and worry about them. Archie Goodwin, for example, does Nero Wolfe's leg work. Meyer is an economist who can explain complicated business and financial matters to Travis McGee. Hawk opens doors into Boston's criminal netherworld for Spenser. Police officers have their snitches and their fellow officers. Reporters have their sources.

The growing and shifting relationships between sleuths and their acquaintances help define them and make them human and accessible to readers. These secondary but important characters offer material for the subplots that deepen and define your sleuth, who may, for example, be a bold and decisive investigator but a hesitant and flawed lover, or who may find himself torn between family commitments and the demands of his investigation.

Relationships and interactions among friends, family members, lovers, business associates, and even rivals will help to define and complicate and individualize your sleuth and add texture to your story. If secondary characters do none of these things, they don't belong there.

Minor characters

Some characters appear once or twice to serve specific story functions. The taxi must have a driver. The gangster has his bodyguard. The politician has a press agent, the business executive a receptionist. When you draw these characters on your pages you can sketch them with a couple of quick strokes, since you know they're unimportant.

But wait. Your readers don't know that these characters aren't, in fact, key players. The Senator's press agent could be the one who hired the hit man to bump off the woman who was blackmailing his boss. The bodyguard might turn out to be an undercover police informant. The receptionist might actually be the CEO's mistress.

Shrewd mystery readers trust no one. Everybody's a suspect. They know that a seemingly minor character can turn out to be the villain.

Don't disappoint them.

You can't—and shouldn't—create elaborate backstories for every taxi driver and waitress who accepts a tip from your hero. Don't exaggerate their importance, and don't introduce them for the sole purpose of complicating your plot and misleading your readers. Play fair. You know they're minor.

But recognize every character's potential as a suspect. Make those quick descriptive strokes and snatches of dialogue memorable enough to stick in your reader's mind.

Mystery readers, like writers, enjoy creating and discarding scenarios. Don't deprive them of their fun.

Creating memorable secondary characters

Mystery readers understand that bartenders and secretaries, cousins and stepdaughters, auto mechanics and family doctors—and, in fact, every character who steps onto the page—*could* be a suspect. Readers look for clues to the mystery's solution in these characters. They understand that hastily and carelessly drawn characters, besides being uninteresting, do not make valid suspects. If you ignore the potential of minor characters by making them flat, one-dimensional cut-outs, you will not only write lifeless stories, but you will also deprive yourself—and your readers—of a rich source of suspects.

If all of your characters except the bad guy are caricatures, readers will solve the case too easily. If none of your minor characters is carefully drawn, they will all be instantly eliminated as suspects by discerning readers. In neither case have you fully exploited the opportunity to create the complexity that mystery readers love.

Give even your minor players the depth and texture to be possible suspects. Take care to draw none of them as transparently and one-dimensionally good or bad. Let your readers interpret them with some uncertainty.

The case of the whistling janitor

Your protagonist enters the lobby of an office building, looking for information. He notices a janitor. Who would know the people who work in this building better than a janitor? Who would be in a better position to have seen or overheard things that can help your sleuth?

At this point, your shrewd reader thinks, "Yes, and who would have a better opportunity to commit crimes here?" Your janitor thus becomes an instant suspect if you introduce him cleverly. Only you know for sure whether he's a red herring or the actual villain. Be careful not to give it away too easily. Let your reader wonder about this janitor.

You might proceed this way:

> A janitor wearing a starched gray shirt and matching pants puttered nearby. He looked about seventy. He was short and wiry, with iron-colored hair slicked back tight against his scalp and white stubble sprouting on his cheeks. He chewed an unlit cigar butt with his stumpy gray teeth. He had sad brown eyes and shaggy eyebrows and a long nose that looked as if it had been broken a few times.

Inexperienced writers tend to confuse detailed physical description with deep characterization. In this passage, the writer draws a clear picture of the janitor's physical appearance. But it is a flat, one-dimensional, rather typical portrait that opens no window into the man's character or life.

He's a cliché who offers no surprises, no different from the bubble-headed blonde, the whore with the heart of gold, the wine-guzzling panhandler, or the unscrupulous used-car salesman. Readers yawn at clichéd characters. They've met them before.

Some writers go to the other extreme, writing exaggerated physical descriptions in their effort to create memorable minor characters. They might introduce our janitor this way:

> A janitor wearing a Hawaiian shirt and plaid Bermuda shorts puttered nearby. He was barely five feet tall and weighed at least 300 pounds. He sported a Fu Manchu mustache, and his scalp had been shaved to the skin except for a strip down the center, which was dyed purple and hung behind him in a long ponytail tied with a pink ribbon.

Grotesquely obese (or emaciated) waitresses, seven-foot (or five-foot) lawyers, and purple-haired (or skull-shaven) teenagers, or characters who are incredibly beautiful (or ugly), smart (or stupid), graceful (or awkward), do not strike the reader as true-to-life. At best, they're utterly boring; at worst, they make the narrator or point-of-view character (and, by extension, the author) seem superficial and mean-spirited, and they will alienate rather than attract the reader.

Complicated and interesting characters can be created with quick and simple strokes by giving readers something they don't expect. For example:

> A janitor wearing a starched gray shirt and matching pants puttered nearby. He was pushing a big canvas basket on wheels. He bent close to me and emptied an ashtray into his basket. He was whistling softly.
> "Pachelbel," I said.

He turned. "Huh? You talking to me?"

"The canon by Pachelbel," I said. "It's what you were whistling. Can I talk to you for a minute?"

Major characters can—and should—be developed gradually. But writers need "tags"—quick, deft, unexpected strokes—to bring minor characters to life. A janitor who whistles classical tunes while he sweeps the floor, a beautiful actress who bites her fingernails, or a professor of Renaissance literature who carries a confession magazine under his arm will etch themselves indelibly in your readers' memories.

These characters are established and ready to be more fully exploited if and when you choose.

Remember: In real life, we learn more about people through how they behave and talk than by how they look. How people appear, in fact, is often deceiving; the same is true of fictional characters. If you focus on your characters' speech, mannerisms, actions, and responses to situations in the story, you won't need to paint detailed physical descriptions of them or make them look strange for them to be memorable.

Avoid the trap of telling readers what to think about a character. Instead of calling a cab driver "grouchy," show him acting grouchy through what he says and how he behaves. Don't call a woman "flirtatious"; instead, show her flirting with a man.

Mystery readers want to figure it out for themselves, and they resent a writer's depriving them of the opportunity to draw their own conclusions about characters. The writer's golden rule— "Show, don't tell"—is never more important than in creating interesting minor characters.

Secondary characters play a limited but crucial role in your story's development. You needed that whistling janitor to give your hero vital information, or to tell him the location of a businessman's office, or to direct him to the fire escape. He's a player. He might have a bit part, but without him the story will not work. He deserves your attention.

Some minor characters, of course, are simply walk-ons. They are the bus drivers, ushers, clerks, waitresses, and others who anonymously populate your story. They serve a function, and should be thought of as objects rather than characters. If a bartender's only function in your story is to deliver a drink, don't describe him or give him dialogue. Just call him "the bartender," as you'd call a passing vehicle "an automobile." Characterizing him further is not playing fair. It intrudes on your narrative and distorts it by suggesting that the bartender might be more significant than he really is.

Playing Mr. Potato Head

When my children were little, they had a toy called Mr. Potato Head. It came with plastic noses, ears, mouths, hats, moustaches, hairpieces, and glasses that they'd mix and match, sticking them onto a potato to create a face.

To create memorable minor characters, try playing Mr. Potato Head. Draw your characters from your experience. Mix and match the mannerisms, life experiences, and appearances of your friends and the people you encounter. Take note of how people around you act and react, speak and behave. Observe their table manners, reading habits, gestures, expressions. What do they watch on television? How do they spend their free time? What do they read, sing, and drink? How do they dress and wear their hair?

Don't seek bizarre combinations or you will create cartoons rather than believable characters. Encourage your reader to wonder about them and care about them. Don't present too much information; choose a few details, then allow your readers to use their imagination to create their own interpretations.

Why, for example, does that actress bite her nails? Did her parents mistreat her? Does her husband abuse her? Is she afraid or insecure or guilt-ridden?

Does the English professor with the confession magazine actually read it? Does he write confessions under a pen name? Is vital information coded into one of the magazine's stories?

And the janitor who whistles Pachelbel—were his parents classical music lovers? Was he—or is he—a serious musician? Did an accident, or an enemy, or a cruel trick of fate deprive him of a career as a concert violinist?

When a quick sketch prompts your readers to ask questions such as these, you've done your job.

Chapter 5

Point of View: Giving Your Reader a Place to Stand

The next time you find yourself in a crowded restaurant, take note of which sense impressions have registered on your consciousness. Perhaps you've tuned into the restrained argument between the young couple at the next table. Your waitress has a bawdy laugh and an engagement ring on her left hand. From the direction of the kitchen comes the aroma of sautéed garlic, which conjures up ancient memories of your grandmother's kitchen and reminds you that you skipped lunch.

Now ask your dinner companion what she notices. The Vivaldi they're piping in through the speakers is nice, she says, but the clank and clatter of silverware and crockery are terribly annoying. What about the waitress? Oh, she wears too much makeup and her roots are showing. The smell of garlic? Now that you mention it, it is a little unpleasant, isn't it?

You and your dining companion bring different memories, interests, sensitivities, moods, and expectations to the simple experience of sitting in a restaurant. Each of you notices different things. Your reconstruction of the evening is therefore radically different from that of your friend.

You can report it only as you experienced it—from your own point of view. That's why eyewitness accounts of events often conflict wildly with one another. For a great many reasons, all of us perceive and interpret things differently.

Of course, in reconstructing your evening at the restaurant you could also recount your dinner companion's impressions—but only as she chose to share them with you. You probably wouldn't know why she chose to be critical of the waitress' grooming or why she failed to notice the argument at the next table, although her facial expressions, gestures, tone of voice, and body language might give you clues. Perhaps she was jealous of the attentions the waitress received from her male customers. For all you know, your friend was eavesdropping but didn't want to admit it to you.

You experience your life only through your own point of view. Part of that experience, of course, comes through your interactions with others. But you can never crawl into other people's heads and experience what they experience, nor can you trust their reports to be entirely accurate or complete. People lie, distort, omit, and otherwise fail to say exactly what they really think. You must impose your interpretations on what others tell you, basing your conclusions both on what you know or infer about them and on your own preconceptions about human nature. In your interactions with others, you must rely on your own point of view.

In fiction, events are filtered through the five senses of the point-of-view characters and then reported to the reader. Establish your story's point of view immediately—preferably in the first sentence. Let your readers—the participants in your story's puzzle-solving quest—know whose shoes they will be walking in as they move through your story, whose eyes and ears and nose they'll be using to witness your story's events. Choosing your story's point of view is one of your most crucial storytelling decisions.

First person

The first-person narrator is the character who experiences the events of the story and who interprets and explains them to the reader in his or her own words.

Kinsey Millhone, for example, is the "I" in Sue Grafton's popular mystery series. Readers walk—and sometimes run—through the stories in Kinsey's shoes. They go only where she goes, know only what she knows, see and smell and hear only what she experiences and is aware of and believes is important. Readers don't know what any of the other characters is thinking or feeling or experiencing. They can only speculate based on what the characters say and how they act in Kinsey's presence.

Grafton begins *A Is for Alibi* by immediately establishing Kinsey's first-person narrative voice:

> My name is Kinsey Millhone. I'm a private investigator, licensed by the state of California. I'm thirty-two years old, twice divorced, no kids. The day before yesterday I killed someone and the fact weighs heavily on my mind.

The very first word in Grafton's book is that first-person possessive pronoun "my," clearly establishing the first-person point of view. Kinsey is straightforward and candid from the beginning. Readers trust she will tell them the truth, and they have faith that she will share important information with them.

Through the eyewitness reports of the first-person narrator, readers accumulate information. They test it, interpret it, link it with other bits of information, and formulate theories. Readers understand that things are happening offstage that Kinsey cannot tell us, and they assume that the story's other characters do not share all of their thoughts with her. Some characters, in fact, may mislead Kinsey. Others could be lying.

First-person narrators are not omniscient. As a young female California private investigator, Kinsey Millhone has her own ways of perceiving the world. She notices and understands things differently from the way John D. MacDonald's first-person narrator Travis McGee and Sara Paretsky's V. I. Warshawski do.

Readers who want to solve the case must take into account Kinsey's personality and limitations as well as the facts as she recounts them in her narrative.

It's no coincidence that so many successful mystery stories are told by first-person narrators. Readers readily identify with the "I" of these tales; it's a powerful alliance. If readers like and trust the first-person narrator, they feel that they have a friend. It makes for strong reader loyalty.

Readers meet and learn about other characters directly through the experiences and perceptions of the first-person narrator. For example, early in Linda Barnes's *A Trouble of Fools*, Carlotta Carlyle's doorbell rings:

> It was slightly past noon on a late September Sunday that had no business being so cool, and I wasn't expecting anybody. I squinted my left eye shut and pressed my right one to the peephole. If I had been expecting someone, it wouldn't have been the cozy old lady who perched on my front stoop like an inquisitive bird. As I struggled with the last deadbolt, always sticky, she turned up the collar of her woolly pink coat, and got ready to hit the buzzer again. She wore white cotton gloves. I haven't seen a pair of white gloves in ages.
>
> "Coming," I yelled, forestalling the buzzer.
>
> She was too old for a Mormon missionary, so I steeled myself for the Jehovah's Witnesses pitch. Possibly Antivivisection. I hoped she was antivivisection. I wondered if I could keep a straight face while I asked her where to donate the parakeet for lab research.
>
> She had sparse white hair, like powdered sugar frosting on her pink scalp, and a round face that must have been cheerful when she smiled. Her skin was crosshatched with fine lines. Deeper ridges creased her forehead and carved channels from her broad nose to her small anxious mouth. Her gray eyes, unsettlingly steady, stared gravely at the peephole.
>
> The lock gave, and I yanked open the door, apologizing. She didn't respond like a proselytizer or a fundraiser.

"Margaret Devens," she announced hopefully. "Miss," she added. "Miss Margaret Devens, spinster."

In this passage, readers meet Margaret Devens through Carlotta's eyes, just as they might meet any person in real life. They form impressions based on what Carlotta observes and what Miss Devens chooses to say. Readers know only what Carlotta is thinking and feeling. They cannot enter Miss Devens' mind. The self-proclaimed spinster may subsequently prove to be a terrorist, or a kidnapper—or an antivivisectionist. But readers won't know that until Carlotta does.

Readers must respect the first-person narrator. She must be at least as intelligent and observant as they are if the puzzle-solving quest is to challenge both reader and narrator equally. Mystery readers do not want to solve the problem while the hero or heroine is still muddling around gathering clues and acting confused. First-person narration works best when the narrator is actively engaged in the story's quest. Give your sleuth reasons to go places, to witness events, and to have a variety of experiences. Her narration, as much as possible, should be firsthand and immediate. A passive sleuth such as Nero Wolfe (who rarely leaves his Manhattan apartment) would make a poor first-person narrator, as author Rex Stout realized. That's why Stout gave the narrating job to Archie Goodwin, Wolfe's gofer.

Suspense develops when narrators find themselves in trouble. They sometimes take risks, miscalculate, underestimate the danger of a situation, and confront a desperate adversary. Readers, identifying with the first-person narrator, accept her danger as their own.

But don't ever try to convince your readers that your first-person narrator might be killed. They know she survives. After all, she's lived to tell about it.

Third person limited

Closely related to the first-person point of view is the intimate, or limited, third-person narration. With the substitution of the third-person pronoun "he" or "she" for the first-person "I," the effect is almost identical. Readers identify only with the single viewpoint character. They know that that character—and only that character—is thinking and feeling and experiencing.

In her novel *The Sculptress*, Minette Walters introduces readers to Rosalind Leigh, the third-person narrator, as she awaits her prison interview with a convicted murderess:

> Rosalind Leigh, waiting by the door of the interview room, ran her tongue around the inside of her mouth. Her revulsion was immediate as if Olive's evil had reached out and touched her. *My God*, she was thinking, and the thought alarmed her, *I can't go through with this*. But she had, of course, no choice. The gates of the prison were locked on her, as a visitor, just as securely as they were locked on the inmates. She pressed a shaking hand to her thigh where the muscles were jumping uncontrollably. Behind her, her all but empty briefcase, a testament to her lack of preparation for this meeting, screamed derision at her ill-considered assumption that conversation with Olive could develop like any other. It had never occurred to her, not for one moment, that fear might stifle her inventiveness.

In this third-person passage, readers share the point-of-view character's thoughts and feelings just as intimately as if it were a first-person narration. The effect for readers is identical and equally powerful.

In the limited third-person narration, just as in first person, readers meet secondary characters through the eyes of the point-of-view character. Here's how Thomas Harris, in *The Silence of the Lambs*, introduces Jack Crawford to readers through the point of view of Clarice Starling:

> She found Jack Crawford alone in the cluttered suite of offices. He was standing at someone else's desk talking on the telephone and she had a chance to look him over

for the first time in a year. What she saw disturbed her.

Normally, Crawford looked like a fit, middle-aged engineer who might have paid his way through college playing baseball—a crafty catcher, tough when he blocked the plate. Now he was thin, his shirt collar was too big, and he had dark puffs under his reddened eyes. Everyone who could read the papers knew Behavioral Science section was catching hell. Starling hoped Crawford wasn't on the juice. That seemed most unlikely here.

In this passage, Harris manages to tell readers as much about Starling as about Crawford. Sharing her thoughts and feelings, readers learn that she is "disturbed." By her casual use of an analogy, readers know that she understands baseball. Her familiar reference to "Behavioral Science section" pegs her as an insider. She remembers how Crawford looked a year ago—a hint that they are acquaintances, but probably not close friends.

Harris scrupulously avoids telling us more about Crawford than Starling knows or observes. He thus does not violate the limitations of the intimate third-person narration.

When describing another character or an event through the third-person point of view, you might be tempted to step back and offer more information than the viewpoint character can know or observe. Don't do it. It's intrusive and confusing, and it destroys your reader's close identification with your point-of-view character.

Inattentive writers, for example, might construct a scene this way:

> Michael Blake took a deep breath and pushed open the glass door. He was worried, and a frown creased his handsome face. He saw Sarah Benjamin sitting at the patio table. Her glasses were perched low on her long aristocratic nose. She was reading some old letters from her missing daughter. She wore a bulky sweatshirt for warmth against the autumnal chill and an old pair of

baggy blue jeans that had fit her snugly before the chemotherapy. Her ordeal had etched a few more wrinkles in her craggy face, but otherwise Blake thought she looked the same as ever.

Notice what happens here. The passage begins in Michael Blake's point of view (he "took a deep breath and pushed open the glass door"). Readers know his feelings (he "was worried"). So far, so good. But abruptly the eager writer intervenes to tell the reader that Blake frowns and that his face is handsome.

Think about it. When you frown, are you thinking of the expression on your face, or that it's "handsome"? No. You are thinking about whatever it is that causes you to frown. You would report what you see and how you feel—but not what your own face looks like. By describing Blake's face, the writer's own point of view takes over the scene, and the intimate third-person point of view has been destroyed.

Then readers are told that Sarah Benjamin is reading "old letters from her missing daughter." Can Blake see what she's reading from where he stands? Does he know who wrote them? No. The writer has intruded again. And then the writer proceeds to explain why Sarah is wearing a sweatshirt and even a bit of the history of her jeans—details which Blake, the ostensible viewpoint character, could not know.

Point-of-view violations such as these make readers feel schizophrenic. They become acutely aware of another point of view—that of the writer, who is manipulating these characters. Thus the intimate bond between the reader and the point-of-view character is broken.

A point-of-view trick

At the end of the first chapter of your mystery novel, your first-person narrator says: "I should never have answered the phone that night. I should have wrapped a pillow around my ears and let it ring. Little did I know that Chloe's seemingly innocent request would nearly cost me my life."

The transparent "little-did-I-know" foreshadowing trick is commonplace in first-person and limited third-person mystery stories. It seems to create suspense, saying, in effect, "Keep reading. There's an exciting story awaiting you."

Actually, unless the little-did-I-know device is used subtly and with restraint, readers will recognize it as a cheap trick. It betrays the insecurity of the writer who doesn't trust his own story to tug his readers forward. When the narrator says "little did I know," he is also saying, "Now I do know, but I'm not going to tell you yet. You've got to read this book to find out." Thus the narrator is admitting that he does not intend to be entirely candid with the reader, and the strong narrator-reader bond of trust is weakened.

A variation on the "little-did-I-know" trick occurs when the narrator introduces a piece of evidence and then refuses to describe it to the reader for several pages. For example: "Between the pages of the old family Bible I found an envelope. With shaking hands, I tore it open and slid out a single piece of paper. I read it slowly. Then I sat down, lit a cigarette, and read it again. I felt beads of sweat form on my forehead."

At this point, of course, the reader expects to be told what is written on that piece of paper. The narrator knows, and the reader trusts her.

But instead, the scene continues: "I folded the paper thoughtfully and slipped it into my purse. It answered a lot of questions. I stood up, stubbed out my cigarette in the heavy glass ashtray, and went to the telephone. It was time to talk to Charles."

By now, the frustrated reader is asking: When is she going to tell me what's written on that piece of paper?

The writer is trying to create suspense, and it's a valid technique provided it's done with restraint. For example, readers will not object if the point-of-view character reads the note to Charles over the telephone. But if she has a conversation with Charles in which she still fails to divulge the contents of the paper, and if she then gets into her car, drives to her lawyer's house, has a discussion with him, and proceeds to confront several other characters, and still does not explain what's written on that all-important piece of paper, readers will begin to feel betrayed by this point-of-view character whom they've trusted. They will resent her coyness. She has key information that she's not sharing, and readers will correctly feel that she has violated the mystery story's rule of fair play.

Multiple point of view

In the suspense stories of writers such as Barbara Michaels and Ken Follett, the whodunit puzzle, if it exists at all, is usually secondary. The question that propels the plots of suspense novels typically asks: Will the good guy succeed in preventing the bad guy from completing his evil plan?

Suspense stories, thrillers, and other mystery subgenres derive their tension less from a puzzle than from the uncertainty of the outcome. There's a contest between good and evil, and readers follow the play of both sides. They turn the pages to find out who wins.

Sooner or later, readers generally learn who the villain of a suspense story is. As often as not they spend time in his or her point of view. The question is not the villain's identity or motivation. Rather, the problem that drives the suspense plot is whether this villain will succeed in his plan to assassinate the President, or blow up the chemical factory, or kill more archeology students. Will the heroine stop him in the nick of time? Will she manage to find out where the kidnapped child is being hidden before the bomb explodes? Will the villain kill the heroine's brother?

Suspense can be enhanced by alternating the narration among the points of view of several different characters. In *The Silence of the Lambs*, for example, readers witness most of the scenes from Clarice Starling's viewpoint. But Harris heightens the suspense of his story by periodically showing scenes from the point of view of other characters, including the victims, the evil Dr. Lector, and Jame Gumb, the story's villain.

If you're writing a mystery story in which the central quest involves solving a puzzle, however, stick with a single point of view. First person or third person. Your choice. Don't be tempted to tell your reader what your other characters are thinking and feeling by entering their viewpoints. That will divide your readers' attention and blur their identification with your sleuth.

There are, of course, exceptions. Tony Hillerman, for example, masterfully alternates between two intimate third-person points of view in his mystery novels. But Hillerman is a master, and his series features two more or less equal protagonists, Joe Leaphorn and Jim Chee. Most successful mystery writers, however, stick to the single point of view. Beginners should do the same.

Besides blurring your readers' identification with your sleuth, the multiple viewpoint also creates tactical problems in puzzle-driven mystery fiction. When writers alternate point of view among several characters, readers inevitably know more than the story's sleuth. They have the advantage over her, which violates the rule of fair play just as surely as if vital information were withheld from readers.

Here, for example, is a scene as it might be told from a secondary character's viewpoint (Sarah Benjamin) rather than the story's sleuth (Michael Blake):

> Sarah peered over the tops of her glasses and watched Michael push open the glass door and step tentatively onto the patio. She saw a frown crease his handsome face. Poor Michael, she thought. He was a nice guy, but he didn't know any more about how to deal with a dying old woman than anyone else.
>
> She shivered. Even in her bulky sweatshirt, she was cold. She was always cold. The chemotherapy had sucked all the warmth from her body. In spite of what the doctors told her, she knew she'd never be warm again.
>
> Or perhaps it was rereading Mary Ann's old letters that gave her the chills.

Well, maybe Michael would help. She hoped so. She didn't know where else to turn.

He'd resist, she expected. He'd protest that he was a lawyer, not a private eye, that he was overworked as it was. Dear Michael. She knew that he'd rather go golfing. She'd have to handle him carefully.

Here readers know things about Sarah that Michael, the sleuth, can only surmise. Through Sarah's point of view readers learn that she intends to "handle him carefully." They know that she will attempt to manipulate him. Michael, at best, can only deduce this important fact.

At this point in the story, readers might legitimately consider Sarah a suspect. Once they hear her thoughts and share her feelings, however, they know that she should be deleted from their list of suspects, because if she had committed the murder, it's reasonable to assume that she would be thinking about it. Readers are disappointed that the complexity of the mystery is thus reduced.

Suppose Sarah actually is the villain?

Writers who enter the point of view of the villain either cheat inexcusably or give the puzzle's solution away. Fair play demands that no point-of-view character can lie to readers, or deceive them, or withhold crucial information from them. Obviously, uppermost in the murderer's mind are that he did the deed, that he desperately wants to get away with it, and that people are trying to bring him to justice.

To have him not think these thoughts is cheating your reader. On the other hand, if he does share these thoughts with readers, they will solve the mystery puzzle before your sleuth does.

Writing in the point of view of all significant characters except the villain will also give away the mystery to observant readers. They will notice whose point of view you are avoiding, and they will figure out why.

Omniscient point of view

The omniscient narrator is the author himself, who knows everything and who shares—and withholds—information from the reader as she chooses. This kind of narration, unless handled with great care, feels arbitrary to readers. They tend to feel manipulated by it. They know they are being told only what the writer chooses to tell them. The puzzle feels like a game of hide-and-seek between writer and reader, rather than a problem for the reader to share with a sympathetic sleuth.

Here is a version of our earlier scene between Michael Blake and Sarah Benjamin, this time told from the point of view of an omniscient narrator:

An anxious smile creased Michael Blake's handsome face. The tall, middle-aged lawyer pushed open the glass door. He was wearing a pin-striped suit. A thin leather briefcase dangled from his hand. He looked at the old woman sitting at the patio table. Her glasses were perched low on her long aristocratic nose. She was reading old letters from her daughter. Sarah Benjamin hadn't seen Mary Ann since the death of her husband, Mary Ann's father. All she had left were these faded old letters.

Blake was not only Sarah's lawyer. He was also her friend and confidant. He wasn't sure why she had summoned him. He knew she was dying of cancer. Probably she wanted to straighten out her will, settle things while she was still able.

"Sarah," he said to her, making his voice as gentle and friendly as he could under the circumstances.

When she heard Michael's voice, Sarah peered up at him over the tops of her glasses. She shivered. In spite of the bulky sweatshirt—it had once belonged to Mary Ann, a souvenir from their summer trip to Quebec back when Charles was still alive—she was cold. It was the damned chemotherapy.

With this omniscient narration, the reader wanders more or less randomly into and out of the heads of the two characters. Sometimes they are seen from a distance as they are described by the author. At other times the reader is privy to their thoughts. Readers are given no shoes to stand in except those of the all-knowing writer, and they are being asked to identify with two characters simultaneously.

Except in highly skilled hands, omniscient narration feels manipulative and impersonal. Even when it manages to sustain a complex puzzle, it discourages readers from caring about it or trying to solve it.

The neutral or missing point of view

A variation of the omniscient is the point of view that consistently keeps readers at arm's length from all the story's characters. The all-seeing narrator reports only what is observable and refrains from entering any character's mind.

The neutral narrator reports the Michael Blake-Sarah Benjamin scene this way:

> Michael Blake pushed open the glass door. Sarah Benjamin was sitting at the patio table. Her glasses were perched low on her long aristocratic nose. She was studying a stack of papers. She wore a bulky sweatshirt and baggy blue jeans. There were deep creases in her craggy face.
>
> "Sarah," said Blake gently.
>
> She raised her eyes over her glasses without lifting her head. "Well, hello, Michael," she said with a soft smile. "Come sit."
>
> He went over and sat across from her. She held her bony hand to him and he took it.
>
> "You've been avoiding me," she said.
>
> "Nonsense," he replied.

In this example, the creases in Sarah's face and her bony hand simply describe her. They no longer work to hint at Michael's fondness for Sarah or his concern about her deteriorating health.

Unlike the omniscient, the neutral point of view is really no point of view at all. Because it forces readers to observe each character through a one-way mirror and prevents them from entering any character's mind, they are unlikely to care deeply about any of them.

Second person

In the second person, the narrator is someone called "you." Instead of a character being the story's protagonist and narrator, "you" are.

For example:

> You take a deep breath and push open the door. You see Sarah sitting at the patio table. She's not looking well, you think.
>
> "Sarah," you say.

With this point of view, you hope to convince your reader to become a character in your story. But readers *know* they're not pushing open doors and speaking to Sarah.

Avoid the second-person point of view, if only because it's so unusual that it calls attention to itself. It strikes the reader as a facile stylistic trick. To be effective, writing should be invisible. It should allow readers to submerge themselves in the story by identifying with a single sympathetic character. Second-person narration keeps reminding readers that they're being toyed with by a writer who's trying awfully hard to be clever. It gives them no character to connect with.

A short story might sustain a second-person narrator. But I know of no mystery novel that's done it successfully—or of any serious writers who'll admit that they've even tried.

Chapter 6

Setting: The Scene of the Crime

No matter what your sleuth is doing—driving a car through the night, interviewing a suspect, waiting in an office, getting beaten up, watching television, or lying in bed thinking—she always has to be somewhere.

You can't have a scene without a setting.

Setting is more than place

Setting is more than geographical place. It comprises all the conditions under which things happen—region, neighborhood, buildings, interiors, climate, weather, topography, flora, fauna, time of day, season of year. It involves not just the scenery, but also the sounds and smells and textures of places.

Successful mysteries have been set in every imaginable city and region in the world. Big cities such as New York, London, Boston, Detroit, and Los Angeles are popular. Sara Paretsky has put Chicago on the mystery map. But increasingly such writers as Tony Hillerman and Jake Page are invoking the richness of the American Southwest. Carl Hiaasen and Edna Buchanan are among the many who set their mysteries in Florida. Dana Sabenow writes about Alaska and Patricia Cornwell about Richmond, Virginia. Philip R. Craig's novels take place on Martha's Vineyard; Brendan DuBois writes about New Hampshire's few miles of seashore. All of these settings work because the authors know them. What's really important is being so familiar with your settings that you can invoke the defining details that will bring them to life and be useful in your stories.

Your settings must strike your readers as realistic. A true-to-life setting persuades readers to suspend their disbelief and accept the premise that your story really happened. The easiest way to do this is to write knowledgeably and confidently about real places.

Mood, theme, and character

Mystery writers appeal to all of their readers' senses to establish their story's setting and mood. James Lee Burke, in *Black Cherry Blues*, evokes a section of Baton Rouge this way:

> The rain clattered on my truck cab, and the wind was blowing strong out of the southwest, across the Atchafalaya swamp, whipping the palm and oak trees by the highway. West Baton Rouge, which begins at the Mississippi River, has always been a seedy area of truck stops, marginal gambling joints, Negro and blue-collar bars. To the east you can see the lighted girders of the Earl K. Long Bridge, plumes of smoke rising from the oil refineries, the state capitol building silhouetted in the rain. Baton Rouge is a green town full of oak trees, parks, and lakes, and the thousands of lights on the refineries and chemical plants are regarded as a testimony to financial security rather than a sign of industrial blight. But once you drive west across the metal grid of the bridge and thump down on the old cracked four-lane, you're in a world that caters to the people of the Atchafalaya basin—Cajuns, redbones, roustabouts, pipeliners, rednecks whose shrinking piece of American geography is identified only by a battered pickup, a tape deck playing Waylon, and a twelve-pack of Jax.

In this passage, Burke's narrator focuses on his physical surroundings—the colors and sounds and the people who are part of the place. Although Burke does not directly describe any sense impressions other than "clattered" and "thump," it's easy to smell the refineries and chemical plants and to feel the dampness of the southwest wind that blows in from the swamp.

In a film or a stage play, the setting is always visible to the viewer, and conversations, actions and setting are available simultaneously. Complex settings do not distract from other components of the scene. In a book or short story, however, all that's visible is what the writer presents in words. A powerful paragraph of description such as Burke's does not interrupt the story's flow. Longer—or less adept—descriptive passages, on the other hand, can cause readers to lose touch with the story's characters and action.

The writer's challenge is to integrate setting into a scene's other components, such as dialogue and action, so that it is vivid without interrupting or intruding on the events. Here is how Sue Grafton's narrator, Kinsey Millhone, describes the motel she has just entered, in *F Is for Fugitive*:

> I moved to the counter and peered to my right. Through an open door, I caught a glimpse of a hospital bed. There was the murmur of voices, but I couldn't see a soul. I heard the muffled flushing of a toilet, pipes clanking noisily. The air was soon scented with the artificial bouquet of room spray, impossibly sweet. Nothing in nature has ever smelled like that.
>
> Several minutes passed. There was no seating available, so I stood where I was, turning to survey the narrow room. ...

Here the descriptions are short, so that the reader's attention remains on Kinsey. The smells and sounds of the motel are carefully woven into the scene without distracting readers from their focus on Kinsey and her reason for being there.

Opening scenes with setting

Films typically begin with an "establishing shot." The camera pans across a crowded restaurant or a mountain range or a city street to fix the viewer in a place *before the action begins*. Coming at the beginning, establishing shots do not interrupt ongoing action or distract the viewer.

Mystery writers can use the establishing shot to equally good effect. The following passage, for example, begins Chapter One in Peter Hoeg's *Smilla's Sense of Snow*:

> It's freezing—an extraordinary 0-degree Fahrenheit— and it's snowing, and in the language that is no longer mine, the snow is *ganik*—big, almost weightless crystals falling in clumps and covering the ground with a layer of pulverized white frost.
>
> December, darkness rises up from the grave, seeming as limitless as the sky above us. In this darkness our faces are merely pale, shining orbs....

Here Hoeg uses an establishing shot of the dominant element in the setting, the snow. Then he pans quickly to the cemetery ("the grave") before establishing that other people ("our faces") are present in the scene.

Lawrence Sanders begins *The First Deadly Sin* this way:

> There was quiet. He lay on his back atop a shaft of stone called Devil's Needle, and felt he was lost, float- ing in air. Above him, all about him stretched a thin blue sac. Through it he could see scribbles of clouds, a lemon sun.
>
> He heard nothing but his own strong heart, the slowly quieting of his breath as he recovered from his climb. He could believe he was alone in the universe.
>
> Finally, he stood and looked around him. Waves of foliage lapped at the base of his stone; it was a dark green ocean with a froth of autumn's russet. He could see the

highway, the tarred roofs of Chilton, a steel ribbon of river uncoiling southward to the sea.

Sanders' opening scene, like Hoeg's, depends largely on description. But neither of the scenes is static. Something is happening. In Hoeg's beginning, the narrator's distinctive observations, plus her use of an unusual foreign word, draws readers into the story that will unfold. In the scene by Sanders, readers are acutely aware that the scenery is being presented through the eyes of the point-of-view character, who has just climbed to the top of this rock. Besides establishing specific seasons and locations, both scenes introduce readers to the characters' narrative voices and, by their observations, give hints about their personalities and interests. The two scenes also establish certain expectations in the reader and set the tone for what follows. In this way, even relatively straightforward narrative descriptions, when presented through the point of view of the protagonist, can serve many purposes.

It's not a good idea to postpone the action until you've set the stage in every scene. You might want to open with a snatch of dialogue or a glimpse of a character. But you must quickly give the reader a sense of where and when the scene is occurring. You can integrate a fuller description of the setting into the action of the scene later, so that the separate parts of the scene work together unobtrusively.

Here, for example, is the way Eileen Dreyer begins the prologue to her novel *A Man to Die For*:

> Control your impulses, her mother had always said. Stifle your urges, the church echoed. She should have listened. The next time she had an urge like this one, she was going to lock herself in a closet until it went away.
>
> "Honey, why are we here?"
>
> "I have to make a stop before I take you home, Mom."
>
> A stop. She had to report a crime. Several crimes. That wasn't exactly a run to the local Safeway for deodorant.

Gripping her purse in one hand and her mother in the other, Casey McDonough approached the St. Louis City Police Headquarters like a penitent approaching the gates of purgatory. It seemed amazing, really. Casey had been born no more than fifteen miles away, but she'd never visited this place before. She'd never even known precisely where it was.

A stark block of granite that took up the corner of Clark and Tucker, the headquarters did nothing to inspire comfort. Brass grillwork protected massive front doors and encased traditional globe lamps that flanked it. ...

In this opener, Dreyer uses four short paragraphs to introduce two characters and to create a feeling of urgency before letting readers know where the scene takes place. Delaying significantly longer could risk making readers feel disoriented.

Making settings authentic

You *must* get actual places precisely right. One sour note and you risk losing your reader's trust.

A friend once recommended that I read a book that was set in Boston. In the first chapter was a reference to Newbury Street—except it was spelled N-e-w-b-e-r-r-y. This writer can't be trusted even to get place names right, I thought. How can I believe this story?

I closed the book and didn't pick it up again.

Making settings absolutely authentic requires research. No matter how many times you've been there, it's a good idea to go back to the places you intend to write about. Observe the people, listen to the sounds, sniff the smells, absorb the colors and textures, talk with the people you meet. Note the vivid images that define the place. Look for the striking details that make it unique and distinctive and that will enable you to bring it to life for your readers.

Here's how Patricia Cornwell leads her readers into a morgue in *Cruel and Unusual*:

Inside the morgue, fluorescent light bleached the corridor of color, the smell of deodorizer cloying. I passed the small office where funeral homes signed in bodies, then the X-ray room, and the refrigerator, which was really a large refrigerated room with double-decker gurneys and two massive steel doors. The autopsy suite was lit up, stainless steel tables polished bright. Susan was sharpening a long knife and Fielding was labeling blood tubes. Both of them looked as tired and unenthusiastic as I felt.

Visiting your local morgue may not be your idea of fun. But it's necessary if you want to describe it with the authority that Cornwell has here. Don't rely on your imagination or what you've seen on television to give you the telling details or the smells and sounds of a place. If it's worth writing about at all, it's worth getting absolutely right.

In many cases, researching settings is not unpleasant. For example, you should make it a point to eat in every restaurant you write about, no matter how familiar it already is to you, at least twice—once just before writing the scene to fix it in your mind, and once again afterward to make sure you've gotten it right. This is not hard work.

Invented settings

Don't feel limited to using actual places if doing so will alter the story you want to tell. An invented setting can still ring true for your readers. Ed McBain fabricated the 87th Precinct and the city where it lies. Katherine Hall Page invented the Massachusetts town of Aleford, and Sue Grafton's Santa Teresa is a fictional place, too. Those who write about actual places commonly invent restaurants, businesses, and residences in them. Readers will readily accept the invented places as real provided they resemble actual places.

If the setting you need exists, use it; if it doesn't exist, make it up, but make it true.

Milieu

In addition to all of the physical elements of place, setting includes the cultures and professions and other activities of your characters. Horse-racing lore is as much a part of Dick Francis' novels as the racetracks themselves. Forensic medicine is a vital part of the settings in Patricia Cornwell's stories. Police procedure is integral to the settings in the works of William Caunitz, Joseph Wambaugh, Ed McBain, and other writers whose main characters are police officers. Sports such as professional baseball and college basketball have served as background for novels by Robert Parker. The traditions and ceremonies of the Navajos are important in the reservation settings in Tony Hillerman's stories.

A setting can be another historical time. Steven Saylor's short stories, for example, take place in Caesar's Rome. Ellis Peters' Brother Cadfael novels are set in medieval Europe. Carole Nelson Douglas, among others, writes Sherlock Holmes pastiches set in Victorian London. Max Allan Collins' Nathan Heller series revisits famous American crimes. Robert K. Tanenbaum's Butch Karp, New York City Assistant District Attorney, works in the 1970s. In all cases, the stories are convincing because the authors exhaustively research the historical period they've chosen to write about. A single mistake in the customs, technology, speech patterns, or dress of the times can destroy the willingness of knowledgeable readers to believe your story.

An authentic milieu helps convince readers that your story is real. It can also appeal to readers' curiosity. Everybody likes to learn something new, and when readers can learn while they're absorbed by an entertaining mystery story, they like it even better.

Settings that work overtime

Your setting is more than just a backdrop for the action of your story. The conditions under which the action occurs can actually do double or even triple duty for you. Setting creates mood and tone. The places where characters live and work give clues to their personalities and motivations. Place, weather, climate, season of year, and time of day can cause things to happen in a story just as surely as characters can.

Shakespeare and Conan Doyle understood how setting can establish mood and foreshadow events. The "dark and stormy night" had its purpose, as did the spooky mansion on the remote moor or the thick fog of a London evening. Contemporary writers use thunderstorms and abandoned warehouses and barrooms and the back alleys of city slums in the same way.

Modern readers are sophisticated, however, and writers have to keep up with them. Obvious settings can too easily become literary clichés. If you misuse or overuse them, they lose their punch.

Never underestimate the power of going against stereotypes. Seek subtlety and irony. Murder can be committed anywhere, anytime. When it happens on a sunny May morning in a suburban backyard, for example, or in a church or school or hospital, the horror of it is intensified.

Carefully selected details of setting delineate the characters who populate it. The pictures or calendars that hang on the office wall suggest the interests and personality of the person who works there. Look for the small details that tell readers about a character before they even see him or her: a policeman's desk littered with half-empty styrofoam coffee cups or cigar butts or used tea bags or chewing gum wrappers; the absence of a family portrait on the desk of a corporate CEO; the music that's played on a lawyer's phone line while your protagonist is on hold; a week's worth of newspapers piled on an elderly widow's front porch; a specimen jar containing a smoker's lung sitting on the desk of a forensic pathologist; a bag of golf clubs in the corner of a politician's office; or a stack of old *Field & Stream* magazines on the table in a dentist's waiting room.

In *Billingsgate Shoal* Rick Boyer's oral surgeon protagonist, Doc Adams, visits his friend Moe Abramson:

Soon I was reclining in a two-thousand-dollar belt-ing leather Eames chair, watching the thirty-gallon aquarium. Two cardinal tetras chased each other from territory to territory. Small iridescent schools of neon tetras and zebra dianos winked about under the fluores-cent light. A Mozart concerto hummed and danced in the background.

An office featuring a big aquarium and Mozart's music can reveal as much about a character—even before you meet him—as his dress, manner of speech, or physical appearance.

Compare what Moe Abramson's office reveals about him with what you might deduce about the man whose apartment Carlotta Carlyle enters in Linda Barnes' *A Trouble of Fools*:

I breathed in a considerable amount of air and was surprised to find it sweet. The place was clean. Pat's flat was a shabby affair, Spartan, the final resting place of a fussy old flirtatious bachelor. Probably a virgin. A faded print couch anchored one wall. Blowsy off-white curtains framed the windows. A framed picture of Jesus hung on the wall over the sofa, a crucifix next to it. A threadbare easy chair with a fat dented cushion faced off against a huge color TV. The furniture wasn't arranged with conversational groupings in mind. It was set up for one man watching TV alone.

The secret of a successfully rendered setting lies *not* in piling detail upon detail. Boyer highlights just three details of Moe Abramson's office—the Eames chair, the aquarium, and the Mozart concerto. Barnes focuses on the furnishings in Pat's apartment. And yet in both cases a few carefully chosen details enable readers to color in these settings from their own imaginations.

Think of your settings as characters in your stories. Set-tings need not be passive; they can act and interact with your characters. Rainstorms cause automobile accidents. Snowstorms cover footprints and stall traffic. The bitter cold of winter kills homeless people in a city park. Water released from a dam raises the level in a river and drowns a trout fisherman.

As you plan your stories, your setting may, at first, be vague and arbitrary. The storyline usually comes first, since it involves character, conflict, motive, detection, and resolution. But as the story begins to grow in your imagination, you'll discover that you need to place it somewhere specific, and as that happens, you'll think of ways that the various elements of setting—place, weather, time of year, and so forth—can give your plot its distinctiveness.

For the general storyline, it may be enough to know that a dead body must be found in Chapter One. Once you decide where your tale will take place, however, you should spend time there. Search out particular places where the events in your story can occur. Visit them often enough to absorb their sounds and smells, their colors, their details. Hang around. Talk to the local people. Walk up the alleys.

Learning the skills of observation will make you a better writer. Look at the places you visit through the lens of a camera. Photographs will help jar your imagination when you're at your typewriter or word processor. If you have an artistic bent, make sketches. Carry a tape recorder and record your observations.

As many details as you gather for your setting, however, avoid extended descriptive passages, because no matter how poetic and original you make them, and no matter how much you might admire the elegance of your own prose, these kinds of passages risk becoming self-indulgent. If they're too long, they will stall the momentum of the action and threaten to bore your reader, who is eager for the story to continue.

The key to creating effective settings in mystery fiction lies in finding the few *telling* details that will hint at all of the others. Be spare and suggestive. Look for a water stain on the ceiling or a cigarette burn on the sofa. Note the odor of mildew or the rattle of a loose windowpane. If you find the right details, your readers will draw the conclusions you want them to without losing track of the story itself.

Chapter 7

Getting It Started: Setting the Narrative Hook

The next time you visit a bookstore, do what most fiction writers do in public settings: Watch the people. Find a browser and study the way she selects a book to purchase.

Something compels her to pull a book from the shelf. Perhaps it's the color of the jacket, or a familiar author's name on the spine. Maybe it's an intriguing title. Whatever her reasons, she now holds a book in her hands. She examines the front cover. That may be enough to cause her to replace the book and choose another.

But if she continues to hold onto that book, she probably flips it over and looks at the back of the jacket. If the author's picture or the blurbs that scream "Amazing!" "Irresistible!" "A real page-turner!" don't put her off, she opens the book and reads the "flap copy," which is generally a plot summary designed as a come-on.

So far, all of the bookselling work has been done by the publisher (except possibly the creation of the title, although publishers often reject the writer's title if they don't think it will grab that browser's attention). Of course, if the author has been published before, his or her name alone might be enough to sell the book.

Potential buyers, at least initially, really do judge books by their covers.

But they do not fork over credit cards for book covers. Watch your browser. If she's still holding that book, she'll next turn to the first page, *and she'll start reading.* This is the writer's moment of truth. Now that potential book buyer is judging the author's work. Keep watching her. Does she quickly shut the book and replace it on the shelf? Or does she lean against the wall and turn a page or two, then smile and sigh and tuck the book under her arm? If so, she's hooked.

Editors and agents evaluate manuscripts the same way that browsers evaluate published books. They read the first sentence, fully prepared to stop there. They believe that a dull or awkward or confusing first sentence portends a dull or awkward or confusing book. But if they're not discouraged, they'll read the entire first paragraph—again, perfectly willing to reject that manuscript if they aren't moved to keep reading.

An opening that compels editors—and book buyers—to continue turning the pages is *absolutely essential* for the unknown writer who wants to be published. It's not enough, of course. A good beginning does not make a good book or guarantee a sale.

But the converse can be considered a truth: A bad start virtually guarantees rejection.

The narrative hook

Opening a book is like meeting a stranger. The first impression makes all the difference. How do the first lines greet the reader? Do they smile softly and seductively? Do they open a trap door and drop the reader into a strange and mysterious new place, or do they crack open a window shade and offer a glimpse? Do they charm readers with their wit? Do they reach out and grab the reader by the throat, or do they politely take the reader's hand and invite her to join them? Do they scream of danger and mystery, or do they enfold the reader in a warm and comforting embrace?

Opening lines can be inviting and irresistible; they can also be awkward, offensive, or dull. They are the window to the book's personality. If the book's beginning doesn't hook readers, they will not read on.

Not any old hook will do. Dramatic, stylized, or otherwise attention-grabbing beginnings are effective *only if they draw your reader into the story*. That's why it's called a *narrative* hook.

An effective narrative hook promises a compelling story populated with fascinating characters. You've got only a few sentences—a couple of paragraphs at the most—to make that promise.

Many different kinds of narrative hooks are available to the mystery writer:

1. *The middle of a scene.* The classical device of beginning *in medias res* (in the middle of things), when executed effectively, drops readers into a situation. They will want to read on to discover both how that situation developed and how it resolves itself. By then they will be hooked on the story.

For example, here is how Ed McBain begins *Ghosts*:

> They might have been ghosts themselves, the detectives who stood in the falling snow around the body of the woman on the sidewalk. Shrouded by the swirling flakes, standing in snow three inches deep underfoot, they huddled like uncertain specters against the gray facade of the apartment building behind the slain woman.

Who is this dead woman? What happened to her? Who are the detectives? Can they uncover the mystery of her death? Such questions are implicit in these two opening sentences. The trap door has opened and readers have fallen in. They will read on.

2. *A vivid glimpse of setting.* Readers are generally fascinated with places. A memorable picture of a place will pull readers into the narrative.

In *Billingsgate Shoal*, Rick Boyer's Doc Adams greets his readers:

> Two and a half miles directly offshore from our cottage in Eastham, Massachusetts on Cape Cod, lies Billingsgate Shoal. It appears on nautical charts in a color between that of either land or sea. This is because Billingsgate is a sunken island and is visible only briefly, in all its soggy splendor, twice a day at tide's farthest ebb.

These opening sentences give readers a peek at a place they'd like to know better. The lines work because readers are confident that the narrator knows exactly what he is talking about. The details are precise and specific and absolutely true. Readers feel they are in good hands, and they also believe that the place Doc Adams describes has relevance to the story that will follow. Billingsgate Shoal seems like a vaguely mysterious place. Things can happen there.

Also important is the early signpost that a character has engaged the reader in a conversation. With the phrase "our cottage," Boyer establishes his first-person point of view in the first sentence. So in this brief, rather straightforward descriptive beginning, a great deal is promised. Readers want to hear more.

3. *A tidbit of interesting information.* Tell readers something they probably don't know, and promise them that this information will be relevant to the story that follows. Readers love to learn new things from novels. Here is an example from my novel, *The Spotted Cats*:

> In Zambia the leopard is called *Nyalubwe*. In East Africa the natives call him *Chui*, and farther south he's called *Ingwe*. But everywhere—in Africa, in Asia, in parts of Europe and the Middle East—the leopard is the same animal: a perfect killing machine, the most efficient mammal predator—aside from man—on earth.

This kind of beginning works best when the information is both specific and arcane. Don't tell readers what many of them are already likely to know. The informational opening succeeds when the information itself hints at danger or mystery *and* the narrative voice is confident.

4. *A snatch of dialogue.* Dialogue is immediate. Stories that open with dialogue accomplish several things at once: They introduce the point-of-view character and at least one other; they create an *in medias res* sense that the reader has entered an ongoing scene; they suggest conflict and hint at mystery and drama; and they characterize the players by what they say and how they speak.

Blanche on the Lam, Barbara Neely's Agatha Award-winning first novel, begins this way:

> "Have you anything to say for yourself?" The judge gave Blanche a look that made her raise her handbag to her chest like a shield.
>
> "Your Honor ... I'm sorry. ... I ..."
>
> "Sorry? It most certainly is sorry! This is the fourth, I repeat, the fourth, time that you've been before this court on a bad-check charge. Perhaps some time in a jail cell will convince you to earn your money before you spend it, like the rest of us. Thirty days and restitution!"

In this brief conversational exchange, Neely creates two characters and establishes a problem. It's an efficient and compelling way to begin a book.

5. *A dramatic moment.* Begin at the beginning—the precise moment when the puzzle presents itself. If it happens suddenly, and if its implications are powerful, you will instantly hook your readers.

Here, for example, in the single compelling opening sentence of *Darker Than Amber*, John D. MacDonald grabs his readers' attention:

> We were about to give up and call it a night when somebody dropped the girl off the bridge.

Similarly, Edna Buchanan begins *Contents Under Pressure* this way:

I stopped to listen. So did a detective and several patrolmen, frozen in motion. One cocked his head and held his walkie up to his ear. The morning had started out as a slow news day, but that could change in a heartbeat. It was happening now.

What happens next? Readers will feel compelled to find out.

6. *An appealing narrative voice.* You don't need high drama or clever wordplay or other tricks to capture your readers' interest. Promise them that they'll be keeping good company on their journey through your story, and they'll want to keep reading.

Here, in *A Beautiful Place to Die*, Philip R. Craig's Martha's Vineyard detective J. W. Jackson invites readers to join him:

> The alarm went off at three-thirty. Outside it was as black as a tax collector's heart. Smart me had stopped at the market the night before for doughnuts, so I was on the road as soon as I filled my thermos with coffee. I rattled through Edgartown without seeing another soul and went on south toward Katama. The air was sharp and dry, and the wind was light from the southwest. Maybe it would blow the bluefish in at last. They were two weeks late, or at least two weeks later than the year before. The heater in the Landcruiser didn't work too well, so I was a bit chilly for the first few miles.

It's a quiet, confident, friendly beginning. Jackson, the narrator, is not out to impress us. Come along, he seems to say. Sit here beside me in my Landcruiser. I expect we'll have some fun.

The most dramatic question raised in this opening paragraph is whether the bluefish will be in. There is no hint of danger, no puzzle, no apparent conflict or tension. And yet Craig's straightforward prose lures readers into his story. Readers can't help liking this narrator and his down-to-earth attention to doughnuts and coffee and his car's heater. They look forward to spending more time with him. They are hooked.

The promise of the narrative hook

The simple job of your story's first sentence is to persuade your readers to read the second sentence, which will lead them to the third, and so on. But no matter how catchy, the beginning of your story will fail unless the promises it makes to your readers are fulfilled.

In every opening you make implicit promises to your readers that:

1. Events described in the first scene are relevant to the story that follows.

2. Characters who appear in the opening are significant players in the story.

3. The mood created in the beginning foreshadows events to come.

4. The narrative voice will sustain itself all the way to the end.

5. Conflicts hinted at early will be resolved as the story develops.

6. Themes established at the beginning will be expanded and explored through the story's events and characters.

A flashy, attention-getting opening that fails to fulfill these promises can make readers feel deceived and cheated. Don't promise what you cannot or do not intend to deliver.

Remember: It's not any old hook. It's a narrative hook. The job of the opening is to lure readers into your story. After that, the story must do its own work.

Begin at the beginning—not before

Commonly, inexperienced writers feel compelled to begin their stories with reams of background information. They feel they must share those character biographies they worked so hard to create, or they compose detailed summaries of the events that preceded the story itself. They write long descriptions of setting or some aimless dialogue that is intended to help readers "get to know" the characters.

The story itself may finally get underway in the second or third chapter. But readers may not be there to enjoy it. One of the surest ways to bore readers and cause them to stop reading is to tell them what they don't have any reason to want to know.

You may need to warm up by writing your way to your story's actual beginning. Fine. Do it. Just be sure to delete it once you find the place where your story really starts.

Stories should open at a significant moment. Begin with *characters in meaningful situations*. Readers do not need to know who the characters are, where they came from, what happened to them earlier, or what they want. Readers don't yet care about your characters' previous lives, and they don't need an explanation of what's going on. Not yet.

Never give readers information before they want it. If your opening scene introduces compelling characters in conflict, readers will read on to learn more about them. The promise of fuller understanding is a powerful hook.

Begin at the beginning. Never earlier.

Chapter 8

Structuring the Story: Building Tension

You've done ALL your preliminary work. You've come up with an original idea; your characters live in your imagination; you've decided on a point of view; you've found a vivid setting; and you've sketched out key scenes.

Now it's time to assemble these elements into a plot.

Planning and outlining

Some successful mystery writers are able to start writing a story with no more than an interesting character, a dramatic first scene, a snatch of witty dialogue, a compelling premise, or even just an opening line. They proceed on the faith that what they write will give them impetus to write more, and that the more they write, the more quickly the momentum will build.

It's a process of discovery for them. Their characters say and do surprising things and come to life as they emerge on the page, urging the writer forward.

Those who feel they don't need to know where their stories are going when they begin, who rely on their intuitive judgment, unquestionably have powerful instincts. As the words they have written push them along, schemes and concepts that reside in the fuzzy area between conscious and subconscious thought pull them forward. They develop and refine plans as they write. They need to get their story underway before they can fully imagine it. As they write, their minds begin to buzz with ideas, options, fragments, and images.

Other writers take the opposite approach. They will not write a single line until they have meticulously planned and outlined every scene in the story. They know exactly how the story will begin, how it will build to its climax, how it will be resolved, and how it will end. They know the life histories of all their characters and everything they will do and say. In effect, they finish all the creative work before they sit down to write the first page.

Planning and creativity

For beginning writers of mystery fiction, the most sensible approach emphasizes thorough planning and structuring while welcoming creativity and spontaneity. Think through and carefully organize the shape and development of your story, but always remain open to new ideas as you proceed. If you prefer to work from a long detailed outline, be willing to shift directions and alter it once your story is underway. Nothing fires the imagination like unleashing characters on the page. You should always listen to your imagination.

You can begin writing once you have asked all the "what if" questions, so you know how and why the crime was committed; you have thought hard and long about the dynamics between villain and victim; you know who your key characters are and how each one will either help your hero or complicate his quest—or, in some cases, do both.

At this point, your writing plan is a sequence of several key scenes that proceed according to cause-and-effect logic. These are the confrontations and major turning points that change your story's direction and are essential to its progress.

You know where you're going. You have a destination in the form of a climactic scene where the pieces of the puzzle will come together.

Don't begin writing until you have fully imagined these elements—sequence, the key scenes, and the climax. Write them down, expand them, give them detail. Before you try to write the first line of your story, construct a narrative outline. There may be plenty of gaps—unimagined scenes and bridges that you know must occur between the key plot points, characters you have not thought much about, subplots that you trust will grow organically from your story's central spine.

Outline and plan until you're sick of it. You'll know you're ready to start writing when you cannot bear the thought of planning and outlining for another minute.

By then your first scene is vivid in your mind, and you're eager to get it down on paper. You are confident that you will find the route to your story's first plot point, and from there you'll find your way to the second, and so on to the climax.

No matter how fully you've imagined your scenes or how excited you are about executing them, don't write scenes out of sequence. Let your key plot points work as writing goals for you. Let them pull you forward. They'll motivate you and make you eager to keep writing.

Know where you're going, and have at least a general idea of how to get there. But remain open-minded. Listen to your characters and follow the new ideas that emerge as your story unfolds. Be prepared to follow the new directions that did not occur to you in your original plan.

As you gain experience, you'll develop your own ways of combining planning with spontaneity. You may, for example, write your climactic scene first. Or you may write several key scenes, then fill in the spaces between them with the bridges and other scenes that link them. The more you write, the more likely you will be to develop an approach that combines careful planning with spontaneity. Learning how to take maximum advantage of thoughtful planning without stifling your own creativity comes from practice and experience.

Tempo, rhythm, and pace

Like a complex symphony, effective mystery fiction should unfold in ever-changing rhythms and tempos. It should alternate movements in allegro, andante, presto, and adagio. The tense dialogue scene needs a contemplative bridge before the car chase. The intrusion of the burglar is more dramatic when it interrupts a quiet love scene.

The sequence in which scenes occur must take into account pace and tempo as well as the demands of the storyline. The tense scenes in which Robert Parker's Spenser tracks down and confronts dangerous killers, for example, are broken up by quiet times in the kitchen and tender moments with Susan Silverman. Between interviewing suspects and witnesses, Sue Grafton's Kinsey Millhone goes jogging or visits Rosie's, her neighborhood bar. John D. MacDonald's Travis McGee takes a break from his confrontations with evil men to have a drink with Meyer, his philosophical friend. Many writers use humor to provide relief from suspense.

These changes of pace allow readers to pause, take a deep breath, process what has happened so far, and build up their anticipation for the next conflict. Your story is an experience for your readers. It shouldn't put them to sleep—but it shouldn't exhaust them, either.

Cliffhangers and other momentum builders

Thomas Harris ends a chapter in the middle of *The Silence of the Lambs* in the intimate point of view of Catherine Martin, who is imprisoned in a deep pit in a dark cellar:

> Except for shock and disorientation, it would not have been so long in coming to her. As it was, the skin emollient did it. Skin. She knew who had her then. The knowledge fell on her like every scalding awful thing on earth and she was screaming, screaming, under the futon, up and climbing, clawing at the wall, screaming until she

was coughing something warm and salty in her mouth, hands to her face, drying sticky on the backs of her hands as she lay rigid on the futon, arching off the floor from head to heels, her hands clenched in her hair.

The next chapter begins:

> Clarice Starling's quarter bonged down through the telephone in the shabby orderlies' lounge. She dialed the van.

Catherine Martin is left there, trapped and screaming, for the reader to worry about while the story shifts to Clarice Starling's search. This is a classic cliffhanger.

In multiple point-of-view stories, scenes often end with the hero figuratively (and sometimes literally) hanging from a cliff by his fingertips. Will he manage to crawl to safety before the bad guy finds him and stomps on his hands? Will the heroine get there in time to rescue him before he loses his tenuous grip?

Sorry. He's left hanging there, and the story shifts to the abandoned warehouse, where the heroine finds herself tied to a chair with a time bomb ticking under her. She struggles to untie the knots. The clock ticks away the seconds. ...

The scene shifts again, this time to the villain, speeding across the desert in his pickup truck, pursued by his vengeful former partner. His tire blows out, he skids, his truck careens off the road. ...

And so on. Every scene ends before it's resolved. Provided readers have come to care about what happens to the characters, cliffhangers keep them turning the pages.

Cliffhangers don't work the same way in the single point-of-view mystery. Readers walk only in the shoes of the heroine, who cannot proceed to search for her partner until she escapes from the warehouse. The hero cannot confront the villain until he pulls himself to safety from that cliff.

Some mystery writers, understanding that readers tend to stop reading at the end of chapter, keep them turning the pages by ending their chapters at a tense moment in the middle of a scene. Readers cannot put down a book when a character they care about has only ten seconds to extricate himself from that chair and race out of the warehouse before the bomb goes off. They must see how—or if—he does it. And so they keep reading.

The cliffhanger can be overused. If every chapter ends in the middle of the dialogue, or with the unexpected intrusion of a mysterious stranger, or with the ringing of the telephone, or with a gunshot, readers will begin to feel manipulated. They don't keep turning the pages just to see who says what next, or whether the mysterious stranger is friend or foe, or who's calling in the middle of the night, or whether the bullet hits anybody. They keep reading because they care about the characters, are puzzled by the mystery, and have an emotional investment in the hero's quest.

If each scene does its job, it moves through the stages of goal, conflict, resolution, and new obstacle. It advances the story and creates a new problem for the hero, which builds genuine momentum and suspense and impels readers to move on to the next scene, and so on to the end of the story.

When it's done well, readers will say, "I couldn't put the book down." But if they decide to mark their place at the end of the chapter and turn out the light, that's O.K.—as long as they look forward to picking up your book again.

Cliffhanger chapter endings build short-term momentum. They work best in long complicated scenes—especially near the story's climax. Toward the end of *A Trouble of Fools*, for example, Linda Barnes ends a chapter this way:

> Damn. There was the matter of the bartender. If it was the same bartender, old Billy what's-his-face, and if he remembered me, recalled my questions, my license, my card, I'd be sunk.
>
> Maybe I'd have gone in anyway. Maybe I'd have taken some Pulitzer Prize photos, maybe I'd have gotten zip. I'll never know.

Flashing blue lights appeared out of nowhere, racing up behind me.

Shit. I smacked my horn in pure frustration, pulled over. The cops. Always there when you need them.

Readers are unlikely to stop reading here. But cliffhangers do not create a page-turning frenzy in readers if the story's other elements aren't working. And if those elements are used effectively, you don't need many cliffhangers to keep your readers' attention.

Climax

The climax of a mystery story is the scene in which the key puzzle piece is found, enabling the hero or heroine to identify, confront, and subdue the villain. The final obstacle has been hurdled. The villain is revealed and justice is done.

Effective climactic scenes combine surprise, suspense, and satisfaction. Everything that has come before has led to this moment. Here, finally, the puzzle pieces all come together. The climax cannot be a let-down.

If readers have already solved the mystery, there is no surprise. It's an anticlimax, the sign of a failed story.

A suspenseful climax keeps readers in doubt until its resolution. Does the hero know what he's doing? Has he solved the puzzle correctly? Will the villain escape? Will the hero survive?

A satisfying climax brings together the thematic threads of the story. The puzzle pieces are assembled, the villain is identified and brought to justice, and the hero or heroine triumphs. When the story's moral questions are complex and contradictory, its resolution may be correspondingly ambiguous and ironic. But in mystery fiction, justice is served.

Climactic resolutions to avoid

Your heroine has solved the mystery. She's verified her suspicions, tracked down the villain to his hiding place, and now she confronts him. The problem, of course, is that this villain has killed one or more people as the story has progressed. He has proven to be a worthy adversary for your sleuth—elusive, clever, powerful, skilled, and determined to get away with his crimes.

Meanwhile, you have portrayed your heroine as smart and stubborn and highly motivated to solve the puzzle, but otherwise an average person, someone your readers can easily identify with.

Now she faces this worthy villain. How will she triumph? *Avoid* these solutions:

1. *Deus ex machina.* Greek plays sometimes ended with a character playing Zeus or Apollo or Hera being lowered by ropes and pulleys onto the stage. The god character then overpowered the villain, saved the heroine, and solved all of the other problems that had been created in the play. Greek audiences accepted the intervention of a god in their plays because they believed that the gods actively controlled the events in their own lives.

Few modern readers believe in meddling gods. They will not accept an ending in which coincidence or luck resolves what appears to be an impossible predicament. In western movies, the cavalry arrives just as twelve evil men are about to cut the throats of a helpless pioneer family. In detective stories, the police break down the door just as the villain is about to pull the trigger on the handgun he holds to your heroine's head.

If the arrival of the police or the cavalry or the night watchman or the heroine's loyal German shepherd has been planned, or if the savior's appearance makes sense because you've prepared your reader for it in advance, then it will not appear to be coincidence. If it flows logically from the story, in other words, it can work.

Here are some other examples of unsatisfactory endings that are tantamount to divine intervention: Your heroine, who has no particular experience with guns, kills the villain with a lucky shot; the villain, normally athletic and sure-footed, trips and falls and cracks his head on the corner of a table; an unexpected thunderstorm knocks out the electricity just as the villain reaches for your heroine's throat; the villain's car, in which he's carrying the bound-and-gagged heroine, runs out of gas in front of a police station.

Endings such as these are easy to write but hard for readers to swallow.

2. *The suddenly invincible hero or heroine.* You have created a desperate and resourceful villain. He has outwitted and overpowered and murdered several strong and capable people already. Now your heroine, using, for example, her skills at computer programming, has identified him. When she tells him what she knows, he says he must kill her to protect his secret. Your heroine then subdues him with karate kicks. Unless her karate expertise has been clearly established earlier in the story, this resolution will seem as contrived as the arrival of the cavalry.

3. *The suddenly fallible villain.* The police and the FBI have failed to bring your villain to justice. Everyone who has confronted him has been killed. Now, at the climactic moment, your heroine faces him—and he does something stupid or clumsy that allows her, unlike all those who have previously tried and failed, to subdue him.

This sort of unmotivated change in the villain is as unconvincing as the sudden invincibility of the heroine.

4. *The conversion of the villain.* Your heroine confronts the man who has murdered several people in cold blood. She condemns his evil ways. He nods and says, "You're absolutely right. I'm ready to give myself up. Take me in."

Unless you have portrayed your villain as a morally complex man, perhaps highly religious and tortured by his deeds, his sudden conversion will strike your reader as lucky and coincidental—another variation on the intervention of the gods.

Writing effective and believable climactic scenes requires all of your creativity. There is no formula. Your story's resolution must follow logically from the strengths and abilities and personalities of the characters and from the events that have come before. And yet it must not seem preordained. The climax must bring all of your story's tension and conflict to a peak. It's the moment when the forces of good and evil confront each other. Make it believable, make it logical—and make it a surprise.

Denouement

In the denouement that follows the climactic scene, the mystery's solution is explained and order is restored. Here the stray puzzle pieces are gathered and sorted and the tangled threads are unraveled. All of the confusing and seemingly random events that have occurred, and all of the characters who have appeared in the story, are rearranged into a logical pattern. Subplots and secondary conflicts such as romantic relationships are resolved. The order destroyed by the murder at the story's outset is now reestablished.

In some cases the climax can incorporate the story's denouement. The hero or heroine assembles the clues in a logical way. She tracks down the villain, confronts him, subdues him, and levels her accusation. The villain admits his guilt and confirms the heroine's suspicions. Remaining questions of motive and means and the roles of other characters are answered in the climactic scene.

When the climax leaves significant questions unanswered, however, an additional scene, the denouement, is necessary. Readers are disappointed if the story ends with plot threads left dangling.

Beware of long rambling confessions. In real life, villains don't typically bare their souls to the good guys who best them. Fictional villains shouldn't, either. Avoid denouements in which the point-of-view character—either in question-and-answer dialogue with another character or in narration directed at the reader—explains how he or she figured it all out. The climax should resolve as much of the story as possible, and the denouement should be completed in two or three short scenes.

Remember: The story is the sleuth's quest of detection. When he or she solves the puzzle, the story is effectively over.

Prologues and epilogues

A prologue is usually a short, focused, single scene showing an event that occurred before the time in which the story itself unfolds. Similarly, an epilogue concerns events that occur after the story's climax and denouement.

A prologue and an epilogue can give symmetry to a mystery, but they can also make it appear that the writer is striving to be "literary." If you are tempted to add a prologue and/or an epilogue as an afterthought, scrutinize your reasons. Most well-told stories don't need either.

A story about an escaped convict who murders the jurors who sent him to prison ten years earlier, for example, might benefit from a prologue in which the convict's original crime is dramatized. If the storyline involves the murder (or was it suicide?) of a disabled Vietnam veteran, try a prologue that recounts the circumstances under which the vet was wounded.

In Rick Boyer's *Pirate Trade*, his narrator, Doc Adams, explains in a prologue called "Lightship Purse" the origin of the baskets crafted by Nantucket natives and the significance of the ivory medallions on their lids. The reader needs this information to understand the story that follows.

James Lee Burke opens *Black Cherry Blues* with a dream sequence that establishes the foreboding mood of the novel and introduces the reader to the tortured mind of Dave Robicheaux, the first-person narrator.

If your prologue sets a mood, reveals a character trait, gives important information, or introduces a theme echoed in the story itself, it is likely to work for you. If it does none of these things, delete it.

Epilogues typically explain what happens to characters after the story has ended. Minette Walters ends *The Sculptress* with this epilogue:

> At 5:30 on a dark and frosty winter morning the Sculptress walked free from the gates of her prison, two hours earlier than the time announced to the press.

She had sought and obtained permission to slip back into society well away from the glare of publicity that had surrounded the release of other celebrated cases of wrongful imprisonment. Roz and Sister Bridget, alerted by telephone, stood outside in the lamplight, stamping their feet and blowing on their hands. They smiled in welcome as the Judas door opened.

Only Hal, sheltering ten yards away in the warmth of the car, saw the look of gloating triumph that swept briefly over Olive's face as she put her arms around the two women and lifted them bodily into the air. He recalled some words that he'd had stencilled on his desk when he was still a policeman. '*Truth lies within a little and certain compass, but error is immense.*'

For no apparent reason, he shivered.

This epilogue, which takes place a significant time after the story itself has ended, is necessary to give the reader a sense of completion. In this case, what happens to Olive Martin after the story itself ends contains a hint of irony and foreboding. The epilogue in *The Sculptress* is dramatically satisfying. It leaves something for the reader to speculate about: Is Olive Martin *really* innocent?

Chapter 9

Building Conflict to
Make Scenes Work

All forms of fiction—films, stage plays, novels, short stories—unfold in an ordered sequence of events or scenes, the purpose of which is to move the story forward. In mystery fiction, each scene is a turn along the maze of the sleuth's journey of detection. If you neglect to account for even one of those turns, your reader will become immediately—and hopelessly—lost.

Every scene should have a function. Test its validity by asking yourself: "If I omitted this scene completely, would the story still make sense to my readers? Would my hero still get to the same place at the end?"

If your answer is yes, you should omit the scene.

While moving the story forward through time and space, scenes perform other functions as well. They introduce new characters. They expand and complicate the personalities and motivations of old characters. They establish setting and mood. They develop subplots, clues, red herrings, and false trails. They amuse, sadden, excite, confuse, clarify, educate.

Scenes dramatize events that are *motivated*. Accident, coincidence, and luck, while common enough in real life, do not move invented stories believably. Readers want to know why events occur. They demand cause-and-effect logic. The law of stimulus-response operates in well-motivated novels and short stories. For everything that happens there must be a reason. Readers may not immediately know what that reason is; in fact, not knowing impels them to continue reading. They trust that explanations will eventually emerge, and they read on, seeking clues that will help them understand the stimuli that produced the responses they witnessed. If those explanations never appear, or if the only explanation is luck or coincidence, readers feel cheated.

Scenes should create the illusion of taking place in *real time*. Action is played out step by step. Dialogue scenes unfold word by word, fight scenes blow by blow, love scenes caress by caress. No significant piece of action is omitted in a scene. As readers witness these events, the illusion becomes their reality. They are there.

You can, and sometimes should, summarize actions: "O'Donnell, the bad cop, questioned the woman for an hour. Then Napoli took over. He played the good cop. He got nothing out of her, either." Or, "They scratched and punched and pulled each other's hair, and then the two women fell to the floor exhausted." Or, "We kissed and stroked each other long into the night."

But while summaries do important storytelling work, they do not create the illusion of observed events for readers. Summaries are not scenes.

Every character in mystery fiction, as we have seen, wants something important that he doesn't have, cannot get without struggle, and is willing to take risks to gain. The sleuth, the truth-seeker, struggles to solve the mystery, while the villain does everything he can to escape detection. Every other character has a direct or indirect stake in the story's outcome. Tension and suspense come from characters whose goals conflict with each other.

A scene can be defined as a closely connected sequence of actions in which one or more characters working toward an important goal encounter obstacles, struggle against those obstacles, achieve some kind of resolution, and end up with new problems. The new problems lead to new efforts to achieve their goals, which are dramatized in subsequent scenes, and so on to the climax.

Every scene, therefore, contains GOAL, OBSTACLE, CONFLICT, RESOLUTION, and NEW OBSTACLE. Eliminate any one of these elements and your scene falls flat.

Let's analyze a typical scene in mystery fiction, this one from *The Sculptress* by Minette Walters. Roz, a writer and the story's protagonist, has agreed to write a book about Olive Martin, a convicted murderess. Roz visits Olive in prison and then does some background research on the unspeakably violent murder of the woman's mother and her sister. Roz is repelled. She cannot bear the thought of spending more time with Olive and writing about it. She decides to tell Iris, her agent, that the deal is off:

> She seized the telephone and dialled Iris's number. "Have I signed anything on the Olive Martin book? Why? Because I damn well can't write it, that's why. The woman scares the bloody shit out of me and I am not visiting her again."
>
> "I thought you liked her." Iris spoke calmly through a mouthful of supper.
>
> Roz ignored this comment. "I've got her statement here and the pathologist's report, or his conclusions at least. I should have read them first. I'm not doing it. I will not glorify what she did by writing a book about it. My God, Iris, they were alive when she cut their heads off. Her poor wretched mother tried to ward off the axe. It's making me sick just thinking about it."
>
> "OK."
>
> "OK what?"
>
> "Don't write it."
>
> Roz's eyes narrowed suspiciously. "I thought you'd argue at least."
>
> "Why? One thing I've learnt in this business is that you can't force people to write. Correction. You can if you're persistent and manipulative enough, but the result is always below par." Roz heard her take a drink. "In any case, Jenny Atherton sent me the first ten chapters

of her new book this morning. It's all good stuff on the inherent dangers of a poor self-image, with obesity as number one confidence crippler. She's unearthed a positive goldmine of film and television personalities who've all sunk to untold depths since gaining weight and being forced off camera. It's disgustingly tasteless, of course, like all Jenny's books, but it'll sell. I think you should send all your gen—sorry about the pun—to her. Olive would make a rather dramatic conclusion, don't you think, particularly if we can get a photograph of her in her cell."

"No chance."

"No chance of getting a photograph? Shame."

"No chance of my sending anything to Jenny Atherton. Honestly, Iris," she stormed, losing her temper, "you really are beneath contempt. You should be working for the gutter press. You believe in exploiting anyone just as long as they bring in the cash. Jenny Atherton is the last person I'd allow near Olive."

"Can't see why," said Iris, now chewing heartily on something. "I mean if you don't want to write about her and you're refusing ever to visit her again because she makes you sick, why cavil at somebody else having a bash?"

"It's the principle."

"Can't see it, old thing. Sounds more like dog in the manger to me. Listen, I can't dally. We've got people in. At least let me tell Jenny that Olive's up for grabs. She can start from scratch. It's not as though you've got very far, is it?"

"I've changed my mind," Roz snapped. "I will do it. Goodbye." She slammed the receiver down.

This scene moves the story. Roz's reluctance to become involved with Olive Martin is crucial to the story's development. On the other hand, unless she does continue to visit Olive, there is no story. Roz begins with the goal of abandoning the story. Iris, knowing how Roz will respond, cleverly creates the obstacle of readily agreeing and suggests that Jenny Atherton, Roz' rival, can take over the project. Now Roz faces a conflict: If she gives up the project, Jenny will get it; if she continues her interviews with Olive Martin, she will be forced to deal with a person who repels her. Roz resolves the conflict by staying on the project, which creates a new obstacle for her: Now she must continue her research into a story that she finds highly offensive.

The scene does other work besides committing the reluctant Roz to write about Olive Martin. It characterizes Roz as uncertain in her convictions, sensitive and emotional, and easily manipulated—all traits that become important later in the story. The scene emphasizes Roz' powerful response to Olive Martin. And it shows that Iris knows how to get her way with Roz.

The law of stimulus-response motivates the characters in this scene. Roz calls Iris to beg off the project. Iris responds by readily agreeing—which, as Iris expects, causes Roz to respond by changing her mind.

The scene gives the illusion of taking place in real time. It contains no summary of events or condensation of time. The conversation between Roz and Iris is played out in its entirety. The attributions in the dialogue and the descriptions of the characters' actions appear to consume all of the pauses in the conversation. Thus readers sense that it takes them as long to read the scene as it would take actually to witness it.

Building bridges

A work of fiction is not constructed entirely of scenes. Some events should be summarized, as we have seen. The passage of time between events needs to be suggested, and the consequences of a scene sometimes need to be pondered.

The bridges or transitions between scenes take various forms:

1. *Summary of intervening events.* What happens between the scenes may be uninteresting, unimportant, or unproductive.

It does not contain the conflict elements that would make it a scene, but it still needs to be accounted for. In *Cruel and Unusual* Patricia Cornwell simply writes: "I tried Marino and he wasn't home or at headquarters." Nothing more is needed.

2. *Indication of elapsed time.* Whether it's a few minutes, hours, or even months or years, you must keep your readers informed about the passage in time between scenes. For example, in *F Is for Fugitive*, Sue Grafton accounts for a hunk of time this way: "After supper, I snagged a jacket from my room and headed down the back stairs."

3. *Analysis of the ramifications of the preceding scene.* Pause before the next scene to interpret and consider the implications of the scene that has just ended. Periodically in mystery fiction readers need to stop, stretch, and take a deep breath. Things have been moving fast. There's a lot to ponder for both the sleuth and the reader. Before you move forward to the next scene, you should help your readers understand what's happened so far and how the last scene affects the story. Here's how Dick Francis does this in *Straight*:

> Perhaps I had been imagining things: but I knew I hadn't. One could often hear more nuances in someone's voice on the telephone than one could face to face. When people were relaxed, the lower vibration of their voices came over the wires undisturbed; under stress, the lower vibrations disappeared because the vocal cords involuntarily tightened. After Loder had discovered I would be inheriting Dozen Roses, there had been no lower vibrations at all.

4. *Consideration of future actions.* What should the sleuth do next? How can he use what he's learned in the preceding scene? What are his alternatives? Unless you share your sleuth's thinking with your readers, they will feel unprepared for the next scene. In *Skinwalkers*, Tony Hillerman uses this bridge:

Leaphorn put the memo aside. When the more normal working day began, he'd call Largo and see if he had anything to add. But now he wanted to think about his three homicides.

Bridges can be as brief as a phrase or sentence, or they can go on for several paragraphs. Their purpose is to move the protagonist smoothly from one scene to the next. Bridges are not always necessary or desirable, and sometimes you can omit them entirely by starting a new chapter or inserting a line break, then beginning the next scene directly. In many cases you can trust your readers to fill in the gap between the two sequential scenes without explanation. The next scene logically comes next, and readers can follow along without being told what has happened or how much time has elapsed between them.

The bridges that connect scenes are by their nature passive and introspective. They are summaries that come directly to the reader from the story's narrative point of view. They do not take place in real time, and they lack all of the other elements of scenes.

All fiction needs bridges. But keep them to a minimum, keep them brief, and keep them focused. When writing bridges, it's tempting to theorize, philosophize, speculate, recapitulate, rhapsodize, and expound. When you do too much of this, your story's momentum grinds to a halt. Mystery readers don't pick up your book to learn your views on life and love and death. They care about your story's characters and their problems.

Chapter 10

Dialogue: The Lifeblood of Mystery Fiction

Because your sleuth can't be everywhere at once, she cannot witness all of your story's crucial events. If she actually saw the crime as it was committed, of course, then there would be no mystery. For the same reason, she cannot overhear conversations in which the culprit reveals his motives, divulges his plans, or confesses his guilt.

That's why dialogue between the protagonist and other key characters is so important in mystery fiction. Although the hero or heroine must be active and participate in and witness many events firsthand, it's largely through conversations with others that the sleuth (and the reader) gathers clues. Thus the primary method for information-gathering in mystery fiction is the interrogation, although it's rarely a simple matter of asking questions and receiving answers. The sleuth understands that the various people she encounters have their own agendas. Some characters refuse to cooperate. Some become belligerent. Some lie or withhold information. Others distort the truth for their own private, and sometimes subconscious, reasons. These lies and distortions can create new directions for investigation, some of which may prove productive while others turn out to be false trails and dead-ends.

Sometimes characters divulge key information without intending to—information that becomes significant only later, after other clues have been collected.

More than other forms of fiction, the mystery calls upon dialogue to perform multiple tasks, such as delineate character, create conflict, build tension, establish mood, present clues, suggest false trails, and give momentum to the story. An effective dialogue scene can accomplish all of these jobs in a few seemingly simple and straightforward exchanges. Because of the special importance of dialogue in mystery fiction, the writer simply must master the art of recreating conversations that are clear, entertaining, and realistic while performing the vital clue-gathering function.

Writing dialogue that sounds real

The conversations that we engage in and overhear in real life tend to be repetitious, semi-articulate, and boring. Transcripts of such conversations, while authentic, would make tedious reading, and the writer who tries to recreate them literally risks writing muddy and hard-to-read dialogue.

In real life, for example, this is how a woman might try to explain to her male friend that she doesn't want him to spend the night with her:

> "I don't—that is, well, I'm sorry, but...."
>
> "I, um, I mean, you sure? That I can't stay?"
>
> "Well, not, you know, not tonight, I think. Just, not tonight."
>
> "Yeah, well, okay, I guess."
>
> "You do—um, do you understand?"
>
> "Well, I guess not really, I don't."
>
> "It's, like, well, sort of confusing."
>
> "Can you, I mean, why don't you try to, ah, explain it to me, huh?"
>
> "Sure, okay. See, I guess I—well, really, to tell you the truth, I just sort of want to, um, be alone."

This exchange is "realistic," but it's not readable. Effectively written dialogue creates sparse and clear speech that wastes no

words and yet sounds authentic. But simply eliminating the
redundant and inarticulate parts is not enough; it produces flat,
lifeless dialogue.

For example:

> "Not tonight."
> "Okay."
> "Do you understand?"
> "No."
> "It's complicated."
> "Try me."
> "Okay. I want to be alone."
> "You mean, you want to be apart from me."
> "Yes."

It's impossible to read this exchange without losing track of
which character is which, of course, but otherwise this dialogue
is sharper and easier to read. The message comes across clearly,
cleanly, and concisely. But it lacks impact. It fails to suggest the
powerful mixture of emotions that the characters must be feeling—emotions that were more strongly conveyed in the first
version.

One way to correct this is to write dialogue in which the
characters talk about their feelings. They can reassure each other
of their love and tell each other of the pain and conflict they are
feeling. Unless handled with extreme restraint, however, direct
expressions of emotion tend to sound maudlin and overblown
and inconsistent with the characters' personalities. They do not
ring true.

For example:

> "I'm sorry. It hurts me so much to have to say this to
> you. I'm very fond of you. I love you. Don't ever forget
> that. It's been wonderful, what we've had. I'm just very
> confused right now. Please understand."
> "Don't worry about it. I'll be fine. It hurts. A lot. But
> I'll manage somehow."

Here the writer has taken the easy way out by having the characters say exactly what they are feeling and thinking. There is no drama in a conversational exchange that tells rather than shows.

Another form of telling rather than showing in dialogue substitutes highly expressive verbs and descriptive adverbs for the characters' own expressions of emotion:

> "I'm sorry," she murmured sadly.
> "Don't worry about it," he growled through clenched teeth.
> "Tonight I need to be alone," she whispered tearfully. "Just tonight," she sobbed. "Okay?" she asked hopefully.

The characters' emotions in this version are absolutely clear. The expressive verbs ("murmured," "growled," "whispered") and the descriptive adverbs ("sadly," "tearfully," "hopefully") leave no doubt in the reader's mind.

The problem here is that the writer has intruded on the scene to explain what is happening in the characters' minds. The reader is yanked out of the point-of-view character's shoes. The author has intervened to remind readers in no uncertain terms that there is indeed a diligent writer at work, controlling their reactions by telling them what's going on and interpreting it for them—and, in the process, depriving them of the opportunity to gather clues and use their imagination. When that happens, readers don't identify or empathize with the characters; they remain passive observers. The intrusive writer has destroyed the potential emotional impact of the scene by overexplaining it.

Truly effective dialogue, like all writing, must show without telling. It works, like an effective film scene, through pictures and dialogue alone. The writer must remain invisible. What is *not* stated shows as much about the characters as what they say and do.

In addition to the spoken words themselves, dialogue writers have two other tools. The first, attribution, should be used sparingly. Its primary purpose is simply to prevent the reader from getting the speakers confused. Not every statement requires attribution. The most useful attribution is "said" because, in dialogue scenes, an occasional "he said"—*without* an explanatory adverb—works as an invisible signpost. It registers, but does not intrude on the reader's involvement in the scene.

Attributions should be inserted into dialogue where they are least intrusive and noticeable—normally in the *first natural pause* in the spoken sentence. In this way, the attribution contributes to the rhythm of the dialogue without calling attention to itself.

Note how the placement of the attributions is less noticeable and enhances the rhythm better in the second of the following two pieces of dialogue:

"Tonight I need to be alone. Just tonight. Okay?" she said.

I said, "You got it."

Or:

"Tonight," she said, "I need to be alone. Just tonight. Okay?"

"You got it," I said.

The second tool in writing good dialogue is what stage actors call "business," the combination of gesture and body language that are incidental to the main action—the conversation—but that suggest feelings and contribute visually to the audience's understanding of the scene. Actors know that the smallest gesture, if well-timed and carefully chosen, can communicate a great deal, whereas elaborate and overblown gestures and actions are distracting and intrusive. Writers, like actors, should avoid overacting.

In dialogue, a piece of business can be used instead of attribution, thereby doing double duty. In the following example, there is no need for the attribution "she said," because the character's actions make it perfectly clear who's speaking:

She put her arms around my neck and her cheek on my shoulder. "It's complicated."

The judicious use of attribution and business frees the writer from having to intrude on the scene to tell the reader, "There was a long moment of silence," or, "He hesitated briefly before he continued."

Here's how Carl Hiaasen combines sparse dialogue, attribution, and business in what is essentially an interrogation scene in his novel *Native Tongue*:

> Joe Winder wanted to talk about what happened in Tallahassee. "I read all the stories," he said. "I went back and looked up the microfiche."
>
> "Then you know all there is to know." Skink was on his haunches, poking the embers with a stick. Winder refused to look at what was frying in the pan.
>
> He said, "All this time and they never found you."
>
> "They quit searching," Skink said. A hot ash caught in a wisp of his beard. He snuffed it with two fingers. "I don't normally eat soft-shell turtle," he allowed.
>
> "Me neither," said Joe Winder.

Hiaasen manages to convey a great deal about the two characters in this simple dialogue scene without describing them. We sense the tension between Winder, who seeks information, and Skink, who is reluctant to give it to him. The scene is highly visual, yet the reader never loses track of the conversation.

In the following fragment of a straightforward interrogation scene from *A Is for Alibi*, Sue Grafton mingles business with dialogue to create a memorable character:

> "Are you Sharon Napier?" I asked.
>
> She looked up. Her eyes were rimmed with dark lashes, the green taking on an almost turquoise hue in the fluorescent light overhead.
>
> "I don't think we've met," she said.
>
> "I'm Kinsey Millhone," I said. "May I sit down?"

She shrugged by way of consent. She took a compact out of her pocket and checked her eye makeup, removing a slight smudge of shadow from her upper lid. Her lashes were clearly false, but the effect was flashy, giving her eyes an exotic slant. She applied fresh lip gloss, using her little finger, which she dipped into a tiny pot of pink. "What can I do for you?" she asked, glancing up briefly from her compact mirror.

"I'm looking into the death of Laurence Fife."

Some dialogue pitfalls

1. *Windbags.* Avoid rambling monologues, long speeches, and one-sided lectures. Try to keep dialogue exchanges terse and to the point. Never allow the reader to lose track of the setting or of the fact that there are at least two participants in the dialogue scene. If your scene requires one character to talk at length while the other remains essentially passive, find ways to break up the speech. Your second character might interrupt and tell the speaker to get to the point. A waitress might appear to take their dinner order. Or the speaker himself might pause to relight his pipe, sip his drink, or scratch his head.

Eyeball your dialogue scenes. If a page of dialogue is solid print from margin to margin, it's too dense. Break it up. A page of readable dialogue should have a lot of white space and ragged margins.

2. *Crowded scenes.* As a practical matter, dialogue scenes with more than two participants are cumbersome for the writer and confusing for the reader. For one thing, when three or more characters are talking, every statement requires attribution or business to clarify who's speaking. More important, the dynamics among several speakers are multiplied geometrically. Two characters constitute a single well-focused relationship. With three characters, there are three relationships for you and your readers to keep track of. When each of four characters interacts

with the other three, there are six separate relationships to follow, and with five characters there are ten, and so on.

Three-character dialogue scenes can be managed if one of the characters—usually your point-of-view protagonist—plays the role of observer or mediator, thus keeping the focus on the dynamic between the other two participants. In general, avoid dialogue scenes involving more than three characters.

3. *Exposition through dialogue.* In real life, people do not tell each other what they both already know. Your fictional characters shouldn't do it, either. It's not an effective way to feed information to the reader.

For example:

> "You're a big guy," he said. "You must be at least six-two and, what, two-forty? I'm just a shrimp. I'm only five-seven and I weigh one-fifty soaking wet. And you've got all those scars on your face and those mean shifty eyes...."

Or:

> "We've been through a lot together, Joe. You and I were in the Marines together. We trained at Parris Island before they shipped us to Chu Lai in '68. We shared a hooch. We saved each other's butt a dozen times. We took our R and R in Australia. And we fell in love with the same woman. That Aussie, Wanda, from Sidney. The tall blonde who was addicted to crossword puzzles and cocaine. She had that old boyfriend, remember? Pete. Yeah, that was his name. Pete Thompson, the air-conditioner repairman, who...."

Scenes such as these do not ring true. In fact, it sounds like poorly disguised exposition—the writer's crude attempt to convert straight narrative into dialogue.

4. *Bores.* In real life, most of the conversations we overhear—or engage in ourselves—are aimless and mundane. The writer's challenge is to create dialogue that seems true-to-life but is never boring. Strive for wit, irony, and cleverness. Scintillating dialogue

emerges naturally from fascinating characters—and vice versa. Give each of your characters a distinctive speaking voice and style. Remember: Boring dialogue makes boring fiction.

5. *Dialogue for its own sake.* Trying to write clever or amusing dialogue for its own sake, on the other hand, is self-indulgent. Unless your dialogue *advances the story*, readers will quickly decide that those witty characters are talking to hear themselves talk and to amuse each other, and that the writer is just showing off.

6. *Dialect.* Because it requires readers to "translate" it, dialogue heavy with dialect is distracting. It tends to distance readers from the characters and the movement of the plot. Moreover, faithful reproduction of dialect risks parody and can be interpreted as insulting and demeaning.

On the other hand, you can't ignore the fact that some characters speak in dialect and have distinctive verbal habits. The trick is to *suggest* dialect rather than replicate it. For example, let your teen-aged characters begin some (but not all) of their sentences with their favorite throwaway word, "Like." Your Down East lobsterman might mutter "Ayuh" occasionally (but not every time he speaks), and your Midwesterner can pronounce the nation's capital "Warshington." If your city-dwelling African-American character says "ax" when he means "ask" and "yo" when he means "yes," your readers will fill in the rest for themselves.

In the following exchange from *Black Cherry Blues*, notice how James Lee Burke underplays the dialect and speech patterns of the Cajun character Batist:

> "Them people that make the movie, they put it in that box, huh, Dave?" he said.
> "That's right."
> "Then how it get up to the antenna and in the set?"
> "It doesn't go up to—"
> "And how come it don't go in nobody else's set?" he said.

"It don't go out the house," Alafair said.

"Not 'It don't.' Say 'It doesn't,'" I said.

"Why you telling her that? She talk English good as us," Batist said.

7. *Four-letter words.* In real life, some people use certain words and phrases habitually, some only under certain circumstances, and some not to all. For dialogue to be technically realistic, some characters may need to use four-letter words, depending on their personality, their background, and their role in your story.

Most contemporary best-selling mystery fiction includes characters who use this language. Four-letter words help delineate the characters who use them and, by contrast, characterize those who don't.

There are readers, however, who are so offended by certain words that they refuse to read books in which this language appears, no matter how realistically. Writers must choose between the rock of authenticity and the hard place of automatic elimination of sensitive or conservative readers from their fan clubs.

Fine-tuning your ear for dialogue

If editors and readers comment that your dialogue sounds stilted and false, the following exercises may help you to fine-tune it:

1. Read and analyze those writers whose dialogue sings. Ed McBain, Robert Parker, Sue Grafton, Lawrence Block, Sara Paretsky, George V. Higgins, James Lee Burke, and Elmore Leonard are among our contemporary masters. In fact, there are very few successful mystery authors who *don't* write effective dialogue.

2. Listen to films or television dramas with your eyes closed. Try to "hear" the emotions and unspoken agendas of the characters. Visualize their gestures and behavior from listening to their speech.

3. Read your own dialogue *aloud*. Even better, have somebody read it to you. Your ear will pick up the false notes that your eye may miss.

4. Eavesdrop on real-life conversations. Listen for the pauses, hesitations, repetitions, and verbal habits that real people use. Then sit down at your keyboard, close your eyes, and try to "hear" those conversations. First try to reproduce them verbatim. Then edit what you've written, adding attribution and business, until it flows smoothly and sounds authentic.

Sparkling, true-to-life dialogue is the foundation of mystery fiction. The trickiest plot twist, the most dynamic cast of characters, the most vivid setting, and the most hair-raising action will not ring true unless your characters talk like real people.

Chapter 11

Getting It Right:
Rewriting and Revising

When I completed my second mystery novel (the first one having been retired to the attic), I circulated a synopsis and three sample chapters and received my share of rejections. So when the editor asked to see the entire manuscript, I was, naturally, elated, and I shipped it to New York by return mail.

Several weeks later I received this letter: "We think you are a good writer. But you've made several typical beginner's blunders. The plot lacks originality. The story lacks suspense. We knew who the culprit was right away. We can't offer you a contract for your book in its present form, but if you'd be willing to rewrite it, we'd be interested in looking at it again."

Rewrite it? I thought. I had just spent more than a year writing, rewriting, and revising that book until it was, I believed, the very best I could make it.

And now they were telling me it still wasn't good enough.

I read and reread that letter. I had arrived, I realized, at a crisis in my writing career. If I could rewrite the book to that editor's satisfaction, I'd be on my way.

If I couldn't, I would probably never write a publishable novel.

It seemed that clear-cut to me.

It took me a year to untangle the original storyline and rework it, to reimagine the characters, to refine the book's narrative voice, to discard old scenes and to think up new ones. It was the most difficult job of writing I have ever undertaken.

But the new version of my book was accepted and, in due course, published. It even won an award. And since then, I've published nineteen more mysteries featuring Brady Coyne, the first-person narrator of that first one.

Writing the original—flawed—version of that book had been hard.

Rewriting it was agonizing.

But getting it accepted, signing a contract, receiving a check in the mail, and eventually, holding a slick hardcover edition of my book in my hand—all of that was a great deal of fun.

The experience taught me what it meant to be a writer: You must be prepared to sit in front of a keyboard when it's the last thing you want to do, and do it regularly, day after day, for as long as it takes to string together thousands upon thousands of perfectly chosen and ordered words that will grab the reader and refuse to let go.

It's work. Writers are like everybody else. Much of the time they'd rather play than work.

On the other hand, if it were easy, everyone would write books. Most people don't, although a great many people say they would like to, and almost everyone is envious of those who do.

Thousands of unpublished manuscripts languish in desk drawers and attics and closets, and for every one of them there are thousands of first chapters and half-finished novels. Writing is like exercising: It begins with a burst of inspiration and good intentions, but it's sustained through all the pain and self-doubt and imperceptible progress and failure by hard-nosed commitment and steely discipline.

It's a hard job, and there's no avoiding that fact. If you want to write mystery fiction, be prepared for it.

But because it's hard, it's correspondingly satisfying.

Peter De Vries said it all: "I love being a writer. What I can't stand is the paperwork."

On writing well

A mystery story that fails to present intriguing characters, a fascinating world, and a suspenseful and complex puzzle, no matter how well it's written, will rarely be published.

The converse, however, is equally true, especially for the beginning writer: A clever storyline, *unless it's well written*, will not sell a book.

There are exceptions to both of these truths. Marvelous writing occasionally sells flawed stories, and fast-paced page-turners that are executed crudely sometimes get published.

You should derive encouragement from these exceptions. "I can write better than *this*," you should say. Or, "I can create a better story than *this* one."

But never think that agents, publishers, and readers of mystery fiction don't care about craftsmanship. Nowadays few editors have the time or the inclination to fix your verbs, cut your scenes, or sharpen your images. You've got to be your own editor. Take pride in your writing. Examine every word and phrase. A well-written manuscript deprives agents and editors of one reason to reject it.

A detailed analysis of the elements of good writing is beyond the scope of this book. But here, briefly, are some of the important principles of effective mystery writing:

1. Good writing *does not call attention to itself or the writer*. Flowery language, convoluted sentences, and ten-dollar words may cause the reader to think, "My goodness, this writer is awfully clever." But if the writing distracts the reader, it fails to do its job.

2. Good writing *tells the story*. It invites the reader to become immersed in the lives, problems, and goals of the characters. That's its job.

3. Good writing *engages the reader's feelings*. It evokes an emotional response. It makes readers *care* about the story's characters and what happens to them.

4. Good writing comes from *strong, active verbs*. Test the effectiveness of your prose by circling your verbs. How many times have you used "was" and "were" and other forms of "to be," or equally flat and flabby intransitive verbs such as "seemed" and "appeared"? Change them. Convert instances of the passive voice into the active form. In good writing, active verbs make things happen. Inactive verbs shift the burden to adjectives and adverbs, which are inherently passive.

5. Good writing *shows*. It does *not tell*. It emphasizes scenes where events occur. It minimizes exposition, explanation, description, and summary. Instead of telling us that a character is sad or angry or frightened, good writing *shows* us the character's behavior and allows us to draw our own conclusions. *Telling* relies on adjectives and adverbs; *showing* comes from active, vivid verbs.

6. Good writing is *concise and clear and efficient*. It wastes no words. It does its job quietly. As Elmore Leonard advises, "Leave out the parts that people skip."

7. Good writing, in other words, is *invisible*. It appears so effortless that readers don't notice it. Good writing is a sleight-of-hand trick. It gives the illusion of ease and simplicity.

Writers work hard to create that illusion. "Easy reading," said Nathaniel Hawthorne, "is damned hard writing."

After the first draft

Dorothy Parker once said, "I can't write five words but that I change seven."

"Nothing you write," said Lillian Hellman, "if you hope to be any good, will ever come as you first hoped."

Writing a novel or short story is like sculpting a statue. The first draft gives it shape and proportion. But it inevitably needs refining and polishing.

The first revision. Once you've written the first draft of any piece of fiction, put it aside. Work on something else and try not to think about it for several weeks. Then read it over with a fresh eye. Try to judge it the way a reader—or an editor—might. Look for the boring parts, the inconsistencies, the dangling plot threads, the pointless subplots. Try to think about all of the elements that make stories work for readers. You'll undoubtedly have to rewrite some scenes, delete others, and add new ones. Think about tempo and rhythm, plot development, character motivation.

Be alert to inconsistencies and errors of fact. Pay close attention to the details. Fiction readers bring to stories a "willing suspension of disbelief." They want to enter the world you have created, and they are prepared to accept the reality of that world and the characters who inhabit it. But a single error or inconsistency, no matter how small, can destroy that willingness to suspend their disbelief. Mystery readers know their guns and poisons and forensics. Mystery writers must know at least as much as their readers. Never confuse a revolver with an automatic or a shotgun with a rifle or gauge with caliber.

Here are four rules that will help you avoid losing readers because of small errors in detail:

1. When possible, write about what you know. Choose settings where you have lived, or at least visited. Give your characters—especially your protagonists—your own profession and hobbies. Use your life experiences as the basis for plots and character conflicts.

2. When you've got to do research, be thorough. Inevitably, you'll have to explore foreign worlds. Your story will require you to create characters such as medical specialists whose work you don't understand. You'll need to know precisely how a government bureaucracy, or a court, or a hospital deals with a situation that arises in your story.

Library and Internet research, of course, is essential. But take the next step. Solicit the help of professionals. If your story needs a scene with a forensic pathologist, interview a forensic pathologist. Ask her exactly how the situation in your story would be handled. After you write the scene, ask her to read it for you. Encourage her to identify every problem, no matter how minor.

Most people enjoy contributing to the creation of a novel or short story and are flattered to be asked.

3. Don't try to impress your readers. Having completed all of this research, it's tempting to use it all. This typically produces long-winded and pointless passages where you show off all of the fascinating material you've worked so hard to master. Examine these sections carefully and be prepared to cut. Your story isn't a catch-all for everything you know and have learned. If it doesn't move your story forward, the passage doesn't belong.

Sometimes you'll find your story needs a major overhaul on its first revision. Sometimes it just needs fine-tuning. But it will always need something.

The second revision. After you're confident you've got the shape of the story right, and after you've double-checked it for technical accuracy, it's time to put a shine on your manuscript. Go back to the beginning and examine each word and punctuation mark, each sentence and paragraph. Hack away flabby adverbs and adjectives, look critically at every verb, listen to your dialogue. Try for absolute clarity in your prose and delete any self-indulgent flights of literary fancy, aiming to follow Samuel Johnson's advice: "Read over your compositions and, when you meet a passage which you think is particularly fine, strike it out."

Some writers find this polishing process tedious, but most enjoy it. At this stage, you've already done the hard part. You've invented a complicated story and all of its elements. You've assembled all of the elements into a novel-length manuscript. This tinkering and refining is your reward.

When you've finished this final polish, you should believe you have written a perfect story.

Mentors. But, of course, you can't completely trust your own judgment. So when you feel that you cannot possibly improve your manuscript, ask someone else to read it—someone whom you absolutely trust to tell you the truth, an experienced writer and reader who understands the kind of fiction you write, who has a sharp eye and ear, and who knows that you *want* the unvarnished truth. You must not ask for praise from your mentor. You want honest criticism.

Friends and relatives are unlikely to serve as effective mentors. They don't want to hurt your feelings (except for those who might, for various reasons, be eager to take a swipe at your ego). If you're fortunate, you'll know somebody—ideally a professional writer who is also a careful reader and astute editor—with whom you can exchange criticism. If you don't have a mentor, consider paying somebody to criticize your work. It's better to hear criticism from a mentor at this stage, when you can do something about it, than to be rejected by a publisher.

John Irving has said, "It's my experience that very few writers, young or old, are really seeking advice when they give out their work to be read. They want support; they want someone to say, 'Good job.'"

It's *my* experience that those "very few" writers who really do seek advice are the ones who are most likely to succeed. A pat on the back and a hearty "Good job" are not very helpful.

Mentors often see flaws that you can't see because you are too close to your story. Don't automatically and uncritically change everything your mentor finds fault with. But consider all the suggestions and criticisms.

The last word

Now your story is finished. It is, you honestly believe, the best you can possibly make it. You've nurtured it and fought with it, cried with it and laughed at it. It's time to make the final copy and send it off.

It can be a scary time. Erica Jong once admitted, "I went for years not finishing anything. Because, of course, when you finish something you can be judged."

Those living characters, that clever puzzle with all its neat clues, all those vivid places and dramatic events and significant themes that have occupied your consciousness for a year or more—all are abruptly gone. "Writing a book," said Daphne

Du Maurier, "is like a purge; at the end of it one is empty ... like a dry shell on the beach, waiting for the tide to come in again."

Sending off a manuscript can leave you feeling empty. The only cure is to start writing something else. And if your story or novel fails to sell, keep writing anyway. Writers write. Many successful authors have trunks full of early manuscripts they could not—or didn't even try to—sell. If they'd allowed their early failures to discourage them, they never would have kept at it.

Writing is a non-stop learning process. Write regularly and write often. Practice your craft. The more you write, the better you'll become. And when you hold that first copy of your own book in your hand, you'll know that it's been worth every agonizing moment.

Part II

Other Important Considerations

Chapter 12

Writing the Mystery Series

Philip R. Craig

I published my first novel (*Gate of Ivory, Gate of Horn*) in 1969, when I was 35. Then, for 18 years, I wrote novels no one wanted to buy. In 1987 I decided to write one that would sell. You'd think I'd have tried that earlier, but I hadn't; instead I wrote books that I (but no one else) thought were interesting. Hearing of my new plan, my daughter gave me the names of two famous novelists (who will not be identified here) and said,

"Dad, these people make millions of dollars. Do what they do."

Spurred on by her advice, I went to a yard sale and bought two books by each of the writers she recommended. My wife and I each read one.

We didn't like them. My wife hoped we wouldn't have to read another one, but I said, "We're not doing this for fun. It's research. Besides, I've always heard that every writer writes at least one bad book. Maybe, as fate would have it, we just happened to read their bad ones."

So we read the other two books. We didn't like them, either.

The problem was that both writers over-wrote by explaining things that didn't need explaining. For instance, instead of just saying the villain narrowed his eyes as he faced the hero in the showdown, or describing how the femme fatale lowered her eyelids as she faced the hero in the boudoir, both authors gave us a whole paragraph explaining what those expressions meant. They presumed their readers were idiots who couldn't figure it out for themselves.

I didn't plan to copy that technique, but I did notice something I thought might be useful: In both writers' books there was a recurring pattern of events and characters—a formula, you might say. Here it is: [1] The hero is ruggedly handsome, in his thirties, and worldly and competent enough to survive attacks and solve crimes; [2] The heroine is beautiful, bright, in her twenties, and not quite as worldly as the hero; [3] The story is set in an exotic locale such as Cannes, or Istanbul, or up the Amazon River—someplace where, unlike your home town, interesting events might actually happen; [4] There are two plots—the love plot involving the hero and heroine, and the crime plot that might be as simple as murder or as complex as a cartel seizing the oil resources of the Middle East and demanding all the gold in Fort Knox as ransom; [5] There is big money involved, apparently because Americans, in spite of their voiced interest in the poor and underprivileged, are really more interested in reading about the rich and famous; [6] The two plots become entwined and justice and righteousness triumph in the end; and, [7] There is at least one steamy sex scene involving the hero and the heroine.

I told myself that I could do all that, and I did. I made my hero (J.W. Jackson) an ex-cop so he could solve crimes; I created a beautiful woman (Zee); I set the tale on Martha's Vineyard, a place I knew well and which is considered by many to be an exotic locale; I used murder as the crime, since it's never really out of fashion; I threw in a background story about drugs to take care of the Big Money requirement; I tied the love plot and the crime plot together and had justice and righteousness triumph; and, I wrote (badly) a semi-steamy sex scene.

I then found an agent who was willing to look at my manuscript, and to my considerable surprise (remember, I'd spent two decades writing novels that no one wanted to publish), she said she thought she could sell it.

Sure enough, Scribner's bought the book and it hit the bookstores in 1989. *A Beautiful Place to Die*, my second published novel, appeared exactly 20 years after my first one. I was then

55 years old, and I remember joking with my wife: Wouldn't it be great if it was the first book in a series.

I had absolutely no reason to think that would happen, of course. But when I got my first copy of the book, I read this phrase on the cover right under the title: "A Martha's Vineyard Mystery Introducing Jeff Jackson."

A Martha's Vineyard Mystery? Introducing Jeff Jackson? Those words implied more books to come...although no one had told ME about it. That was the first of many times that I have been the last to learn something important about the future of my books.

As it turned out, *A Beautiful Place to Die* was, indeed, the first in a series of novels that have become known as The Martha's Vineyard Mysteries. Scribner's has published the hardcovers, and Avon has published the paperback editions. My agent, Jane Otte, and my editor, Susanne Kirk, have guided and sustained me through the production of a new book every June, so that now, all these years after the publication of *A Beautiful Place to Die*, I may actually be qualified to comment on some aspects of writing series fiction.

To do that I'll refer to my own books and describe how I've dealt with some of the issues I've encountered.

First, a generalization: The author of series fiction must write each successive story in such a fashion that it will be interesting to both first-time readers and those who have read previous entries in the series. The writer must give the new reader enough background information about the characters and setting of the story without boring past readers by repeating too much of what they already know.

Now for some concrete examples of issues:

1. Chronology. You can build the passage of time into your stories, or you can pretty much ignore it. All of Sue Grafton's stories take place about the same time, but Robert Parker's hero, Spenser, grows older with each novel. In my books, time passes, although not as fast as in my life. Whichever way you decide to address the passage of time, be careful to use proper chronology.

Don't make your character 25 years old in one book and 45 in another that takes place the next year. If she gets shot in an early book, she should carry the scar—and the memory—in later ones.

2. Essential information about characters and their circumstances. When you write a series of stories featuring recurring characters, you must give new readers essential information about those characters, but you don't have to tell them everything. In my novels, a cast of regulars has evolved, and when one of them appears, I have to introduce him or her to readers who haven't read earlier books in the series. I do this as briefly and indirectly as possible, and usually only if it makes a difference in the current book.

I make it clear for readers that J.W. Jackson, the narrator of my series, is an ex-cop who retired to the Vineyard to escape police work by having someone—usually someone who wants his help—mention it in conversation.

In earlier books I gave so little information about J.W.'s background that my editor suggested that I provide more. I didn't want to do that all in one book, so I've scattered pieces of his personal history here and there throughout many books. He's a Vietnam veteran who was wounded on his first patrol; he was raised in Somerville, Massachusetts, by his widowed father, who was a fireman killed by a collapsing wall; he has a sister who lives in Santa Fe, etc.

Much of this information appears in the form of internal monologues, since J.W. is the narrator of the books and all of each story takes place in his mind.

He's never been physically described. All we know about him is that he's tall (because he looks down into his wife's eyes); he has big hands (because he puts them on her shoulders); he has big feet (because in one book he was suspected of a crime but was cleared because the perp left tracks and J.W.'s feet were much bigger); and, he's clean shaven (because occasionally he's looked into a mirror and considered growing a beard, although he's always decided not to). We don't know the shape of his face or body or the color of his hair or eyes or skin.

J.W.'s friend John Skye is a university professor of Old and Middle English who is married to a woman with twin daughters by a previous marriage. That information generally comes out indirectly through dialogue or through J.W.'s stream of consciousness.

Zee, J.W.'s wife, was shot in a violent encounter with two gangsters, one of whom she killed. I don't mention that in later books unless it affects the story. The fact that Zee is opposed to guns and violence, yet paradoxically is a marvel with a target pistol, is revealed more often, usually by dialogue ("Say, J.W., how'd Zee do at that pistol competition last week?"), or perhaps by a mention of the trophies she has stacked in a closet.

The point is, you don't have to tell everything all over again in every book. You only have to tell what's important in the current book, and it's best to do it indirectly and minimally.

3. Romance. When I discovered that I was writing a series of books instead of just one, I realized I had a problem: How to handle the love relationship between the hero and narrator, J.W. Jackson, and the beautiful woman, Zee. When I wrote *A Beautiful Place to Die*, I assumed that their sexual union was a one-night stand. But as the series evolved, things changed, and I had to decide what to do with the lovers.

It is conventional for the protagonists in crime novels to be single, so as to be available to new romantic opportunities. James Bond, for instance, has a new girl or three in every story. He was once married but his wife was immediately killed, leaving him once again single and available. Joe Leaphorn, who appears in Tony Hillerman's wonderful novels, is a widower; Bill Tapply's Brady Coyne is divorced; Kinsey Millhone, Sue Grafton's tough West Coast private eye, is twice divorced.

This convention notwithstanding, I realized I liked Zee, so I made a decision: J.W. would continue to pursue her, eventually with marriage in mind. Her reluctance to re-marry (she'd been dumped by her first husband) lasted for four books.

When Zee said Yes in the last line of that fourth book, I began to get letters split about 50-50 between readers who thought marriage was a great idea and those who thought it would ruin everything.

Figuring that I was going to lose half my readers no matter what I did, I hedged my bet for two more books, during which J.W. and Zee were engaged. Finally I made up my mind and married them in the first line of the seventh book in the series. Since then, to further violate convention, they've had two children and stayed married.

I try to keep their romance brewing by the way I characterize them. They love each other, but neither is blind to the other's flaws and foibles, and both are sometimes attracted to others. Since their hormones can act up at inconvenient times, there is a psycho-sexual tension between them that forbids them to take each other for granted.

This tension is increased by J.W.'s refusal to play the role of dominant male—even when Zee wishes he would. Instead, because he holds her happiness higher than his own, he insists that she is always free to conduct her life as she, not he, sees fit. He will not try to keep her to himself; he will only stand between her and other men if she's in danger from them.

Both J.W. and Zee are independent, loyal, loving people, but, as is often the case, their strengths are also their weaknesses. This fact keeps their relationship from being dull, and it ensures that it will remain romantic.

4. Locale. My books all take place on Martha's Vineyard, and the island is so central to my stories that it has almost become a recurring character. It is a paradise with serpents under its rocks, an Eden with trees bearing poisonous fruits. The contrast between its image and its reality is reflected in each story and provides background for the crimes that are the principal focus of the books.

Although I'm careful not to write Vineyard travelogues, I try to describe the island so accurately that both Vineyarders and readers who have never been to the island can see it in their memories and imaginations. I tell islanders of places they may never have seen, and I describe places they know intimately. If I do this well, people who have never visited the Vineyard can see those places, too.

Both sorts of descriptions strengthen the story by giving it verisimilitude. Because my descriptions can be trusted, my story is more believable. Familiar sites, such as the Giant Pagoda Tree on South Water Street in Edgartown, and even the totally fictitious Fireside Bar in Oak Bluffs, give readers the sense that they know the territory. This knowledge pleases them and makes them want to read more.

It is an interesting fact that of the hundreds of letters I get from readers, virtually none of them speaks about the crimes or J.W.'s heroics as a detective. Rather, my readers are interested in J.W. and his family and in my descriptions of the island. They worry and give me advice about the Jacksons. J.W. has been drinking too much beer, they way. It's bad for his health. Or, J.W. shouldn't take his young children with him when he's detecting. It's dangerous. Or, they worry that Zee may be tempted to accept that offer to go to Hollywood. They remind me that I shouldn't have the children stand up on the back seat of the car to give their parents hugs. They should be sitting down with their seatbelts fastened.

Readers also tell me that my descriptions of the Vineyard make them eager to return or to make their first visits. The owner of a local bed-and-breakfast tells me that she gives copies of my books to her new guests so they can find their way around the island. At least a half dozen people have told me they moved to the island after reading one of my books.

These reports and letters suggest to me that by careful, often indirect descriptions of characters, character relationships, and locale, you can write series fiction that is appealing to both new and old readers. The important thing is to provide necessary background information to new readers without boring those familiar with your work.

With this in mind, I try to write each book in my series for a reader who has never read any previous ones. I've been told some readers start with the first and read straight through the latest book; some start with the latest book, and read backward to the beginning, and some read the books in no order whatsoever.

So the plan seems to be working.

Oh! Remember that recurring pattern I extracted from studying the four novels I bought in the yard sale? I followed it in *A Beautiful Place to Die* and then never thought about it again. It's still a good formula, though. You're welcome to try it.

Chapter 13

Standalone or Series Mystery?

Bill Eidson

Okay, you've decided you're going to write a novel. You've locked yourself in your office and you've told your loved ones that you're a busy writer and you're not to be interrupted unless the house catches fire, and then only if the flames are searing *your* door.

By now you've surely thought about the story, the setting and background, you know that conflict is vital, you probably have at least an antagonist and a protagonist in mind.

Question: Is this the first novel in a series? Or are you creating a one-time event in your protagonist's life?

If you truly haven't figured that out yet, it's worth leaving the office and taking a walk around the block, talking to your best friend, or beating yourself about the head with a stick—whatever helps you make a decision. Because choosing between a "standalone" novel or "series" is a decision that will impact every element of your story, including the core idea, characterization, plot, pace, style, and setting. When it comes time to sell the book, it will have a major impact on how the book is purchased and how it will be marketed. It will be one of several ways in which you will be defined as an author, right up there with the sentence-by-sentence quality of your writing.

Now, with that said, did *I* spend much time on that decision?

No.

I didn't know any better.

I knew I wanted to write one story about a character and story idea that I stumbled across, and I went about writing it. It became *The Little Brother,* my first novel. I've written five other standalone books since then, and now I've just written my first novel that I intend to be a series, *The Repo.*

In this chapter, I'm going to focus on the standalone.

Mind you, either decision can be the right one. If you know exactly the kind you want to write, then skip ahead and get started. I'm not going to tell you which one to choose. But if you're still in the consideration stage, I've learned some things that might help you. Maybe you'll make a better-informed choice than I did; maybe you'll just follow your nose and write whatever you want. In the business of writing books, the creative decisions are truly your own.

What is a standalone novel?

A standalone novel is a one-time story. No sequels. No trilogies. The story is truly finished when the reader puts the book down. The reader may be left with an idea about how the characters will live out their lives, but he or she will never get to meet them in print again. In comparison to a series, the structure of a standalone offers the novelist both freedoms and strictures when it comes to the basic elements of storytelling. Let's take them one at a time:

The Idea—I'm going to go out on a limb and state that the core idea of a standalone novel is more vital to its success than it is in a mystery series. Yes, most wonderful mystery novels have great ideas at their center. But the success of a standalone novel is more often dependent upon an idea that makes the reader say, "Oh, it's about X. I've *got* to read that."

Why? Because readers often look to series mysteries for comfort. There may be heinous acts and a wickedly fast pace in a good mystery, but according what I've always read and observed, we go to series mysteries because we like the characters and find them interesting, and we're comfortable with the world the author has created—enough that we want to revisit that world again and again, book after book.

But with a one-time novel we want a challenge. We want a fast ride. We want to believe we're in the scene. The idea of the book is compelling enough to pull us in and drive us hard to the end. We want to see what happens next. Unlike a series novel where we *know* the hero will come out safe in the end, in my own books, anyhow, readers have some doubt. I want them to think, "Maybe this guy *will* lose." Or maybe he'll win over the bad guy, but it will be a bitter victory, given all that he's lost.

The stakes must be high—high for the protagonist, and high enough for the reader to care. This does *not* necessarily mean the world will blow up if the hero doesn't succeed. But whatever is at stake for him must be made real and vitally important to him so that the reader will care.

How do you come up with such an idea? I'll tell you a bit about how I do it. I keep my eyes open to the world around me. I look for points of conflict in "normal" life. I read, I clip news articles. I develop mental muscles the way a photographer learns to "see" a picture. I learn to see story ideas.

Take my first book, *The Little Brother*. Years before I met my wife, I had a blind date with a woman who told me that her roommate was copying her mannerisms, talking like her, and even wearing her clothes when she was out of the apartment. I put that together with an observation I'd made that it was rather strange how people would invite strangers to live with them by placing small classified ads in the "Roommates Wanted" section of the newspaper. Four years of evenings, weekends, and holidays later, *The Little Brother* came out—the same year as John Lutz' *Single White Female*. My book was unfortunately optioned for a movie *after* Lutz' was already in production, so there wasn't much fame and fortune for me.

While you don't hear the term "high concept" these days as often as you did a few years ago, it remains a useful idea. "High concept" means a story that people can recognize instantly as something they'll want to read. The little movie blurbs in the newspaper offer a helpful way to see what a good "high concept" sounds like. One that I remember went something like this: "Two men meet on a train and jokingly agree to kill each other's enemy. Unfortunately, one of them wasn't joking." *Strangers on a Train.*

I taught myself early on to see if my stories could be encapsulated so easily. For instance, my concept statement for *The Little Brother*: "A man adopts the personalities of his roommates and kills them when he feels he can live their lives better than they can. He gets away with it until he moves to Boston and his new roommate and his girlfriend catch on just in time."

Mine was a whole sentence longer than *Strangers on a Train.* Maybe that's why I'm not rich and famous.

The Protagonist—If you look closely, you'll find subtle but important differences in the heroes of series versus standalone novels. For your own story, ask yourself: Whose problem is it anyhow? With the standalone, more often than not the answer should be: "the protagonist's."

Think of it this way. If you're writing a series novel, Mr. X or (Ms. X) walks into the doorway of your detective's office (or caterer's tent, or horse stable, or wherever your protagonist calls home) and lays out his problem. As some sort of expert, your protagonist is supposed to help him out. Yes, she'll make mistakes. Yes, she'll get personally involved. And yes, there may be substantial risk to those close to her as she goes about solving the problem. But initially, the problem isn't hers. She's the expert, she's fully expected to survive and live to deal with other people's problems in the future books.

In the standalone novel, the protagonist more often than not *is* Mr. X. If he walks into a detective's office, either the detective can't help him, or she tries to and fails, leaving the protagonist in an even worse spot. (The movie *Cape Fear* is an excellent example of this.) Often, the protagonist isn't an expert in whatever it is that's threatening him, but he must find the inner resources and expertise along the way to extricate himself and those he loves from the spot he's in.

In many stories, the protagonist is not blameless. He has done something to put himself in a terrible spot and must grow personally during the story to win. In my second book, *Dangerous Waters*, the character finds himself in trouble seemingly from the outside. But decisions he made beginning in his early teens are at the root of what is now happening to him in his thirties.

When I look back at what I've written here so far, I see the words, "Often," and "supposed to," and "maybe" a lot. That's because everything in a good novel is up for grabs. But more often than not, I'm right. The key problem is *supposed to* land squarely on the shoulders of your hero.

The Antagonist—A friend of mine, Frank Robinson, the author of *The Glass Inferno*, which later became the movie *The Towering Inferno*, told me this about thrillers: *Readers measure the good guys by the bad guys.* This means your protagonist can strike all the right poses, say all the right things, and fight with amazing skill, but he's ultimately meaningless if your bad guy is a wimp.

Not to suggest your antagonist must kill everyone he sees, or only wear black leather, or kick puppies for fun. But he must have a certain weight and presence in your story. The reader should feel that his threat is real and that truly bad things might happen to your characters. The reader should understand something about why the bad guy acts like he does. That means you'll have to evoke your readers' empathy (not necessarily their sympathy) so they'll believe that this person might do the thing he does. We've all been assailed by countless snarling bad guys in novels, television shows, and movies. The only way to make yours come to life is to work on the details that make them real.

Usually it's the antagonist's motivation that first drives the story. He wants something desperately enough that he is willing to do terrible things to get it. The protagonist in some way becomes entangled with the antagonist's goals...and that's your story's conflict. So at the heart of your big idea, your high concept, are the characters—the protagonist versus antagonist wanting opposing things.

Viewpoint—I refer to movies as often as books. That's not only because I love movies, but also because I feel that a cinematic viewpoint is helpful for standalone novels. Actually, I feel the same about series novels, which is why *The Repo*, my first in the Jack Merchant/Sarah Ballard series, is written in the third person. I allow readers a limited amount of viewpoint in Jack and Sarah's heads, as well as that of the primary antagonist, Thomas.

Quite often, series novels are told from the first-person POV. I like reading first-person novels (assuming I like the character), but the only book I ever wrote in first person was *Dangerous Waters*. The book turned out well, but I found the first-person point of view constraining. I knew there was a lot of interesting stuff going on with other characters, but I could only relay it through dialogue and other secondhand sources. It drove me crazy. First person offers all sorts of benefits in keeping a mystery a mystery. And it is easier to give the reader an in-depth view of the protagonist's inner thoughts. But I find it more difficult to reveal my antagonist's views in first person. And in most standalones the antagonist is the one driving the story, at least initially.

Think hard about viewpoint. I usually limit the viewpoints to only two to three characters, and I never switch viewpoints within a chapter. One of the benefits of working in third person is that you can choose chapter by chapter which character has the most dramatic or interesting view of the story.

Plot and Pace—With standalone novels, think about a ticking clock.

Is a definite time limit (racing to stop the bomb from exploding, finding the child before she's lost forever) a tried and true device that borders on the cliché? Yes. But it also works. The ticking clock works because it's in the very nature of a thriller. At the most simplistic level, the difference between a mystery and suspense novels is: In a mystery, you want to know who did it. In a suspense novel, you might know whodunit from the first page, but you want to know what happens next.

For the reader to care about what happens next, speed and hard-driving momentum are vital elements of the story. With a good mystery, if your protagonist is engaging, the pace can be more leisurely. But with a suspense novel, if you're not reluctant to put the book down, if you aren't burning to see what happens next, something isn't working.

Think about what's at stake. Think about a short deadline. Think what would happen if even with all the best efforts of the protagonist, that deadline kept growing shorter. Think about making your reader feel anxious. Think about making him give up a night's sleep to finish your book. That's your job.

Endings—With a series, when one story comes to a close readers are comfortable. They know that another will be coming. Better still, they will keep learning about your characters in each new book. So the ending of a series novel is often a matter of tying up the loose ends of the puzzle you've created, restoring order out of chaos, and establishing a sense of continuity with the characters. The pressures and joys your characters encountered in this current story will shape them in the next one. Whatever pains they've incurred and changes they've experienced, they will be available to take on another assignment—in your next book.

In a standalone, the ending is the end of that cast of characters. They are left there forever. You can (and probably should) have them looking toward their future. But since your readers will never see it, you have an opportunity to show your characters as changed forever, if that seems right. In some stories, characters may have lost so much they *should* be changed forever. I have a pet peeve with all the books I've read where entirely horrible things have happened to people and the loved ones around them, and yet they're cheerful at the very end. The dog comes in the kitchen and barks and everyone laughs, as if nothing really happened.

In my sixth novel, *One Bad Thing*, my protagonist has suffered terribly with the loss of his daughter. But he's also taken the law into his own hands more than once, including killing even when he had another choice. I just couldn't think of any plausible reason why he wouldn't go to jail. If he were a series character, I'd think twice. I'd figure something out so I didn't have to send my character off to jail for six years.

But with a standalone novel like *One Bad Thing*, it worked. We see him getting off the bus after he's finally made parole. He's suffered, but there is a faint light at the end of the tunnel, and that's all I wanted. This isn't to say series characters don't suffer. They do, sometimes mightily. But you've got to think ahead and leave them with enough to be ready for the next book.

Movies, marketing, and bookshelf space

Take what I have to say with a grain of salt. To the good, three of my seven books have been optioned for movies. I've seen my books in several different languages, and I've talked about my books on a hundred radio interviews, half a dozen television appearances, and about a dozen feature articles. I've seen a few bad reviews, but all in all, I've received mostly good-to-excellent reviews. All of which is very gratifying.

But I'm also miles away from the bestseller list. None of my books has been actually made into a movie so far. I'm a "mid-list" writer, meaning that my books rank at the middle (or end) of the publisher's sales list.

That said, here are a few things I've picked up along the way about the differences between standalone novels and series books when it comes to movies and marketing.

Movies: Generally speaking, the folks in Hollywood are looking for an idea that has that certain "it" quality which seems fresh...yet familiar. They want a "high concept" idea that is visual in nature. Most of the time we see movies from several different perspectives, even if we're primarily following the action of one protagonist. So more often than not, a standalone novel that is told from multiple third-person viewpoints is more easily translatable to the screen than a series novel told from a single first-person viewpoint.

Character is extremely important to the movie business as well. They are looking for roles that can showcase actors well, so fully developed, appealing characters are vital. Great characters can be found in both standalones and series novels. However, are you willing to sell the rights to your series character based on the sale of one novel to one producer? That's usually what they want. Elmore Leonard says that he's often written about similar characters, but he just changed the names so it wouldn't harm the movie sales. An exaggeration, maybe, but something to think about.

Marketing: There's a notable difference between the marketing of series novels and standalones. With series books, you're looking for continuity. You may or may not benefit from a "honeymoon" in the review press that gives some attention to the introduction of a new series. You may be more likely to get attention in the mystery magazines and more orders from mystery bookstores. With a mystery series, you often start off with the expectation of a "slow sell." This means that the value of your series will be judged by how well your first three books build a following. That's the theory, anyhow. The reality must take into account the computerized inventory systems in the big chain stores that determine your success with that first book—and how many of your subsequent books the chains will buy. So if you sell 3,000 hardcovers of the first book, they'll order 3,200, if you're lucky, the second time. But don't get me started.

The same limitations apply to standalones, except "hitting it big" right out of the box is more important. Why? Because since you are a standalone writer, your next book will have no connection to this one. Both will be judged entirely upon their own merits. The good news is that if you have a truly high-concept idea and a well-realized story, your chances of securing a bigger advance and more publicity are greater than with a series novel.

My fourth novel, *Adrenaline*, was the story of an adrenaline junkie who turned to murder for his thrills. This was back when bungee jumping was big and Nike was running their "No Fear" campaign. I was looking at my own interest in riding motorcycles too fast and thinking how ultimately stupid that was compared with my father's generation, who were sent off to World War II. This was in the mid-nineties when the economy was booming, years before 9/11.

So I worked with my publisher to develop a press release about America's then-current fascination with high risk, and as luck would have it, *Time* magazine did a cover article about the very topic just as my book was coming out in mass market. Even though *Adrenaline* wasn't featured in the *Time* article, we sent the story out along with my press release, and over thirty radio stations across the country signed me up for interviews. We had similar success with my next two books: *Frames Per Second*, about the how digital imaging is changing the credibility of photojournalism, and *One Bad Thing*, about the ten-year anniversary of the largest art theft in the world at Boston's Gardner Museum.

While it's possible that such a nonfiction "hook" can work with a series novel, in a standalone novel it's far more likely to be noticed by the media, which tend to regard mystery series as character-rich whodunits. A standalone novel is more often associated with "the big idea." It will either enjoy a big hit of publicity…or just fade away.

Bookshelf Space: If you ever have the choice between movie options, big publicity, or bookshelf space, pick bookshelf space. You can live without the movies and enjoy a long and successful career, but you *must* have your books on the shelves, along with publicity and in-store push, for them to sell.

If your standalone hits it big, then you might enjoy an enormous distribution in hardcover and mass market with your first book in a volume that few series mysteries ever enjoy until several books down the road. On the other hand, those mass-market books often remain on the shelf for an appallingly short time (30 to 90 days). Then your name disappears until your next book.

In theory, a series book that is well supported by the publisher and the bookstores will maintain your early books (called backlist) on the shelf as each new one comes out. That's great.

When readers come into the store, ideally they'll find your first three books facing out next to your new one. This helps grow your name by the sheer shelf space it occupies, and it encourages people to go back and read your earlier stories. It helps build you over time, which is the primary benefit of a series.

I've got enough series-writer friends to know that theory is not necessarily reality. But the concept is valid. It is one of the most compelling reasons from a business standpoint to write a series novel instead of a standalone.

Making a decision

There are many other differences between standalone and series stories:

The sheer numbers game. I'm referring to the number of times a character can be shot at, kill someone, and lose loved ones without going insane or being thrown in prison. I admire John D. MacDonald's Travis McGee series immensely. That series is one of the reasons I started writing novels in the first place. But poor McGee lost a woman in almost every novel. They'd die some horrible death and he'd avenge them, and I couldn't help thinking that in real life, if you've had about twenty girlfriends die violently, you'd probably feel wary about starting a new relationship.

My point is that over a number of books, you may feel your own credulity strained as you put your series characters through so many paces in one lifetime.

Your familiarity with your characters and setting. This is a big consideration. When I start a new novel with all new characters and setting, I have to spend a lot of time figuring out who the characters are, what they care about, how they'll react to situations, their tone, dialogue style, personal histories...everything. Having started my second in a series, I can see that it's a huge advantage to know the primary characters and setting in advance. This kind of head start can be a limitation, but it has major benefits for the writer.

‹›‹›‹›

Think about the stories you like to read. Think about how you like to write. Think about whether you want to try to hit it big with a standalone or build more slowly, and perhaps more surely, with a series.

Then...do what you want to do. You're the author, after all.

Chapter 14

Seeing Double:
Making Collaboration Work

Hallie Ephron

So you want to collaborate on a mystery novel? You're following a fine tradition. Most famously, there was Ellery Queen, the pen name of first cousins Fred Dannay and Manny Lee, who practiced the art of the classic detective novel from 1929 until Lee's death more than forty years later. Dannay did most of the plotting and Lee did most of the writing. Then there's Per Wahloo and Maj Sjowall, the Swedish husband-and-wife team who wrote the Martin Beck police novels. Supposedly they'd put the kids to bed and write alternate chapters. Today we have "Perri O'Shaughnessy"—sisters Pam and Mary O'Shaughnessy—who often collaborate across an ocean, swapping the lead every other book as they write their series of legal thrillers featuring attorney Nina Reilly.

Cousins, spouses, sisters. Sounds like you have to be related to make it work, but that's not the case. My co-author is my longtime friend, forensic neuropsychologist Donald Davidoff.

It all began in 1996 over the dinner and several bottles of wine that my husband and I shared with Don and his wife. Don, a neuropsychologist, was telling us about a murder case on which he'd consulted as an expert witness. We were fascinated as he told us how he was evaluating an eyewitness, working with defense counsel, and testifying in court. Eyewitnesses, he told us, were notoriously fallible.

"Wouldn't it be neat," one of us said, though I can't remember who, "to write a mystery that hinges on the fallibility of eye-witness testimony."

We started what-iffing, sketching out a plot and characters. By the end of the evening, Don and I had agreed to get together the following Sunday and give it a go. Neither of us had the slightest idea what we were getting ourselves into.

Collaboration styles

Now, with four books under our belts and a fifth one in the works, we're often asked: "Do you *both* write?" Heaven forbid! True, we share the pseudonym, G. H. Ephron. But when we started working together, my biggest fear was that Don was going to want to write. A few months later, he confessed to me that his biggest fear had been that I was going to *make* him write. The collaboration works precisely because we have virtually no overlapping skills. I usually say: "I write. Don *does*."

In fact, he does most of the things our protagonist, Dr. Peter Zak, does. He's a neuropsychologist who runs a unit at a psychiatric hospital affiliated with Harvard; he evaluates defendants in criminal cases and testifies in court; he lives in Cambridge, rows on the Charles River, runs along Memorial Drive, appreciates good wine, and knows all about Mission furniture.

For us, writing together is an iterative and interactive process. We get together once a week to scope out scenes; then I go off and write them. I email pages to Don and he prepares a critique. Then we meet again and move on. Don's insight into psychology, his knowledge of the inner workings of psychiatric hospitals and the criminal justice system, his experiences with ordinary people and those accused of serious crimes—all that makes the books altogether different from anything I could write on my own.

After talking to many writers with successful collaborations, I'm convinced that there are almost as many different ways of working together as there are partnerships. Here are just a few.

You go/I go. Writing alternating chapters and lobbing the manuscript back and forth like a tennis ball, that's how William G. Tapply and R. Philip Craig wrote *First Light*, their first "J.W. Jackson/Brady Coyne Mystery," bringing together their fictional protagonists. They figured out the plot as they went along.

Beginning/End. In this scenario, one partner writes the first half of the book and the second writer takes it to the finish line. That's how Warren Murphy and Richard B. Sapir collaborated on more than forty action-adventure novels, including the legendary Destroyer series. Warren tells it this way: "We'd think up some vague story, and Dick would write the first half of the book and send it to me. No outline, no suggestions, just wonderful characters doing strange things. I wrote the second half of the book, and then, without his knowledge, I rewrote the whole book so it was seamless. Dick never called me on it."

Writing/Rewriting. One partner takes the lead on the first draft, the other revises—this is how Pam and Mary O'Shaughnessy work. They trade the lead, book to book. In the end, Mary says, "It's hard to say who wrote what because we totally rewrite each other's draft. We're both extremely critical of our own work and each other's."

Plotting/Writing. Or, as Paul Kemprecos describes his partnership with Clive Cussler, "He's the storyteller and I'm the writer." The two were mere acquaintances when Cussler invited Kemprecos to collaborate with him on the NUMA Files series.

Togetherness. Some teams do what the rest of us deem impossible: they do it together. Husband and wife team John and Cathie Celestri (Cathie John), authors of two mystery series, actually write each sentence together, though John spends more time at the front end, structuring and outlining the novel, and Cathie does more editing at the back end. Another husband-and-wife team is Mary Reed and Eric Mayer, who write the John the Eunuch mysteries: "It's less like two people each writing half a book and more like the same book being written twice by two people. We tend to allocate scenes according to what we feel are our individual strengths. E's the dab hand at descriptions, for example, while M may write more of the dialogue."

Making it work

Collaborating isn't easy, and more partnerships founder than succeed. "For her it was a hobby that she did in her spare time; for me it was a passion," says a writer whose attempt at a collaboration ended in disaster. "To save myself from getting aggravated because he wasn't working, I wouldn't work," says another author who ended up marooned with a half-finished manuscript.

No matter how the partnership divides the work, there are some constants in those that succeed:

Mutual respect. Each writer has to bring something to the table that the other one values. The ideal writing partner has strengths that fill in the gaps created by the weaknesses in the other's work and vice versa.

Commitment. Writing a novel and getting it published takes a long time. Working with a partner who's in it for the long haul is essential.

Discipline. Collaborate with someone who's going to make the meeting, make the deadline, and do the edit she said she was going to do.

Leave your ego at the door. If you're going to get emotionally attached to your own commas and semicolons, not to mention your words and ideas, then forget about collaborating. It's hard enough to write a good book without your partner having to worry about your hurt feelings.

Keep your sense of humor. Get yourself a writing partner who laughs at your jokes. Humor will get you through the many rough patches.

Hard or easy sell?

Are collaborations any harder or easier to sell? Literary agent Gail Hochman, who represents crime fiction luminaries such as Scott

Turow (and G. H. Ephron), says, "If it's a mystery, no one cares how many people wrote it, but rather if it reads well."

She says a collaboration doesn't deter her from considering a work. It's the promise of longevity that counts.

"As an agent, I want to take on writers who will have a long career—collaborators who can repeat the same kind of success, time after time. A one-shot collaboration is less attractive."

Written agreements

Like most writing teams, Don and I plunged in without a written agreement. Then, to our amazement, we finished our first Dr. Peter Zak mystery. After seemingly endless rejections and revisions, we found ourselves with an agent and a publisher. It was our agent who insisted that we sign a written agreement. It specified that we shared equally the copyright, all proceeds, and expenses. It covered all sorts of contingencies (what if one of us dies? what if the work doesn't get accepted by the publisher? and so on) and included an arbitration clause. Our agent was protecting us, but she was also protecting her literary agency, which was entering into a two-book contract with a publisher on our behalf.

Partnerships (like plots) evolve, so most teams would be hard pressed to come up with a useful agreement that spells out the *how* of working together. On the other hand, writers who've been burned repeat the mantra, "Get it in writing." Never underestimate, they say, the power of money and vanity to undermine a good partnership. The experts agree. Put it in writing, up front, while you're still getting along with each other, and avoid headaches down the road when you're not.

In a standard agreement, two co-authors share the copyright, and each owns one half of the entire work and the proceeds from it. If one person is doing the lion's share of the work, an agreement should be drawn up that spells that out. The Authors Guild advises a flat percentage rather than more complex arrangements.

If one partner's contribution is treated as a "work for hire," then that author receives a flat fee but no royalties or proceeds from the sale of residual rights (paperback, translation, film, etc.). A short written release typically is needed to ensure that the one who commissioned the "work-for-hire" owns and controls the copyright.

The Authors Guild provides collaboration guidelines for writers, as do other professional writers' organizations. Two widely recommended books are *The Writer's Legal Companion* by Brad Bunnin and Peter Beren and *Business and Legal Forms for Authors and Self-Publishers* by Tad Crawford. Both contain model contracts.

Don't wait until the book is finished to decide on your by-line. Many co-authors opt for a shared pseudonym. For us it was a marketing decision. Editors and agents advised us that a single name was easier to remember, and after all, wasn't our goal for G. H. Ephron to become a household name?

If both names go in the by-line, then whose name comes first? And will it be "by Sherlock Holmes *and* John Watson, M.D.," or "by Sherlock Holmes *with* John Watson, M.D.," or "by Sherlock Holmes *as told to* John Watson, M.D."?

Ups and downs

Successful collaborating depends on working with the right person. For us, the synergy comes from bouncing ideas back and forth, from taking turns as cheerleader when the other one poops out.

There have been unexpected bonuses: Sharing the promotional gigs and expenses; taking advantage of *two* networks of friends, professional colleagues, and connections; and the emotional ballast of someone else in the boat with you.

The major downside, of course, is having to split the money. Neither of us has quit our day jobs.

Recently I told Don that sometimes it feels as if I'm collaborating with our character. He laughed and remembered the first batch of pages I emailed him. "I was so surprised. It was like a weird, out-of-body experience, reading about my better half—me, but not me. That's probably the most dystonic piece of all this."

Dystonic? That's the kind of word Don uses all the time. (Dystonic means that something feels odd, not integrated.) And it's just the kind of word our character uses, and then has to explain when the other characters roll their eyes.

"Sometimes it feels as if we share a brain," Don says. "You have the right side, I have the left. Aside from experience, I bring to the table the organization, plotting, and an understanding of people. That's all left-sided. You integrate it all and make these leaps. That's much more right-sided. And the language—language is a left-sided function, but you're using it in a right-sided way."

Using the left side of my brain in a right-sided way? I don't understand this exactly, but it sounds very cool. And besides, I've learned to trust him on just this kind of thing.

Chapter 15

Doing Business with Agents

an interview with Fred Morris

Q: *I've finished my first mystery novel. Why should I try to get an agent rather than submitting it directly to publishers myself?*

A: Now that you've finished writing, you need to shift gears and start thinking about getting your novel published. After the isolation and focus required to get to this point, it can be a difficult mental switch to make, and it can wreak havoc on your self esteem. It's important to keep perspective. Finding a publisher is a process. Unless you are incredibly lucky, you are going to get a number of rejections before you find, if you manage to find, your publisher.

Unless your only goal is to find a small press willing to put out a minimal number of copies, finding an agent, a formidable task in and of itself, is the first step to approaching mainstream publishers. An agent can help you negotiate a deal that will protect you and pay you much more in the long run should your book, and eventually your career, take off.

Many small presses are happy to consider manuscripts by un-agented authors. In some cases the absence of an agent makes their job easier. Small presses are only able to pay small advances, at best. They need to capitalize on their investment by acquiring and exploiting a wider range of rights associated with a book (such as foreign/translation, audio book, and movie rights), which an agent will fight to retain for you. Smaller houses may also pay lower royalties and try to tie up the rights longer than an agent would allow.

Should you find yourself negotiating with a small press without an agent, there are any number of books available to help you figure out what terms to ask for. The Authors Guild offers contract guidelines online. The National Writers Union also provides contract advice to its members.

Aside from some small independent houses, most publishers prefer to receive submissions from agents with whom they already have relationships. Editors are deluged with material to read, and, as is true of nearly everyone in publishing, *no one* has enough time to deal with everything that lands on his desk.

It's a sad fact that thousands of mysteries are written every year which will never make it to the shelves of your local bookstore. In many cases, agents make the first cut.

If you think your book could draw the interest of readers other than your immediate family and friends, and if you want to find a mainstream publisher willing to invest in you and your book, looking for an agent is the best way to start.

Agents will give you their unbiased opinion on the value of your manuscript, but it is only *their* opinion. Any number of factors can come into play in their response to your manuscript. Give it time. Look for agents who work with similar projects.

The harsh reality is that publishing is, without question, a business. Agents make their living by taking a commission on all the money that comes in from the deals they make. Whatever their personal response to your manuscript might be, their actions, and whether or not they are willing to make an investment of time and energy in working with you, will be ruled by their professional assessment. It's an agent's business to be tuned into what kind of books publishers are currently looking for and to have the insight to know what kinds of books will draw a readership even before a publisher has picked up on it.

An agent is the person who's in your corner, even after ten publishers have turned you down.

Q: *How can I figure out which agent to submit my novel to?*

A: There are lots of ways to start the process of finding an agent. Ideally your introduction will distinguish you from a host of other writers. Take comfort in the fact that a well-written query letter with a professional appearance always stands out. Still, the more immediate the connection, the better. If you know a writer who has an agent (and who's happy with that agent), that's a good place to start. Writers workshops and conferences sometimes invite agents to give consultations, and they also give you an opportunity to network with other writers who might be able to make an introduction. If you can get a few one-on-one meetings with agents at a workshop, it's a perfect opportunity not just to pitch your book, but also to refine your approach. Whether they express interest in looking at your manuscript or not, don't hesitate to ask them what you could do to present your book better. Perhaps they can help you fine-tune your query letter, or even suggest other agents you might approach.

Other resources with listings of agents and notes on their specialties can be found online and in how-to-get-published books. One place to start is by reading the acknowledgments in mystery novels similar to your own. Often authors will thank their agent. Once you have a name, an online search should yield contact and information on the agent's submission guidelines and preferences.

Q: *Once I've identified a likely agent, what should I send? The whole book? A chapter?*

A: Different agents have different preferences for how they like to receive material. The general practice is to send a query letter with a self-addressed stamped envelope asking the agent if he would be willing to read the manuscript. The query letter should distill your premise into a tantalizing, to-the-point, and easy-to-read single page. Avoid being cute at all costs. If someone can make an introduction for you, all the better. Some writers send email queries. Different agents respond differently. But with the deluge in email nowadays, making the initial contact by email invites instant dismissal.

No agent likes to be cold-called by a writer. You can telephone to confirm an address, in which case you'll very likely be speaking to an assistant. Once you've sent in your manuscript, it's reasonable to call and check on its status from time to time.

After you've sent your manuscript to an agent who has said he'd like to read it, give him a month from the time he receives it, and then check in by mail, email, or phone. The time lag can be considerable, and it might try your patience. It's up to you how much of it you can tolerate. If there's a special reason you'd like to work with a particular agent, you may want to give it more time.

Most agents expect an exclusive opportunity to consider a manuscript. Certainly they need to know if other agents have expressed interest in the material or are considering it. If you should be in the enviable position of having two agents interested in working with you, try to meet them both and get a sense who you would prefer to work with.

Q: *What are agents looking for in mystery novels these days? How do they decide whether to take on an unknown author?*

A: There's no simple answer to this question. Everyone will tell you that publishing is a very difficult business these days. The mystery market is crowded, and new mystery series are hard to launch. But there's always room for something fresh and intriguing. There's always a market for smooth writing, intriguing characters, and original plots. Different agents respond to different material, and different publishers are looking to develop different areas of their list. It's as much about standing out from the rest as it is about fitting in with them. An agent may describe a client as the next Patricia Cornwell, but the fact remains that we already have a Patricia Cornwell. What agents and publishers both want is a client who can sell like Cornwell, not write copycat mysteries.

All agents want serious writers as clients, writers who will keep writing good books. An agent may be impressed with an author's first effort and want to keep working with that author in the future even if her current book goes unsold. So take note of who expresses interest in you.

Q: *If an agent decides NOT to take me on, does that mean my book is unpublishable?*

A: In the face of the mounds of rejection letters you might receive from agents, let me give you a little encouragement. *You only need one agent.* And remember, different agents have different tastes and different time constraints and different methods for identifying new clients. You simply have to keep working through the process of finding an agent, all the while trying to refine your approach to selling yourself. It's very sad to think of someone who has approached every agent known to mankind with the same lackluster, formulaic, bad query letter only to receive the same form letter saying thanks, but no thanks. Give it time. Get advice where you can find it. Try to distinguish yourself from the rest, and keep writing. When you're ready to quit trying to place your book, start focusing on the next one. And when you look for representation for that second book, focus on that book and that book alone. Don't go to an agent with a laundry list of completed manuscripts. It's overwhelming and self-defeating. Unless you have very impressive credentials that will cause someone to take notice of you, all of your books will steal the focus from each other. The agent will take the easiest path out and just say no to all of them.

Q: *Is it acceptable to submit my book to several agents at the same time?*

A: You can submit multiple query letters. Don't get ahead of yourself, though. This isn't a pyramid scheme. Keep your approach personal and specific to that agent. Once an agent is interested, make sure he knows if anyone else has the manuscript. Many agents hesitate to invest time in reading a manuscript if there's a possibility that the material will be snatched away from them at the last moment. Others will accept multiple submissions with the understanding that the author won't make any decisions about representation without checking with them first.

Q: *Do agents do anything besides finding publishers for books?*

A: Agents are your connection to the business end of your book. They use their accumulated business savvy and instincts to develop and pitch your manuscript to publishers for the initial sale. And more importantly, they enable the publisher to do business with you. Editors and people in publishing are reluctant to involve themselves with writers, even ones who they want to publish, if they're not hooked up with an agent. It's the agent's job to explain the ins and outs of publishing to you, to help you make good business decisions, and to advocate for you to the publisher. Having the agent involved takes loads of pressure off the editor, who, as we have discussed, is already grossly overworked.

Beyond negotiating and shepherding the initial deal for a book, agents also have the connections and know-how to explore selling your book to foreign publishers in translation. They have connections to Hollywood if there's the possibility of selling movie rights. They can help you in developing your next book and help you decide when and if it's time to change publishers. Part of knowing which editor and which house match up with a manuscript is knowing who's buying, which publishing houses are stable, and which houses are cutting back. And when your editor unexpectedly quits or gets fired, or any one of a myriad of unexpected setbacks that can happen, it's your agent who holds your hand and picks up the pieces.

Q: *Do all agents charge fees? Should I work with an agent who asks me for money?*

A: Agents generally charge 15% commission on all domestic sales, including film rights, and 20% on most foreign sales. Agents become, quite literally, partners in the business of selling the rights to your material. If you encounter agents who are brusque, or dismissive, or downright nonresponsive, keep in mind that one of their main resources is their time. They don't get paid by the hour, and if a project can't be sold, they make no money. It's partially the nature of this commitment that makes the agent such an effective advocate for a writer. Underlying the relationship is the tacit understanding that the agent is working in his own best interest as well as that of the author.

Editors, for their part, give agented submissions more consideration simply because the material has already impressed someone enough to invest time and energy in its representation.

Do not trust an agent who charges a reading fee. The only fees agents should be charging, besides their commissions, are photocopying and postage expenses for the actual submission.

Many agents have a representation agreement which lays out how expenses will be handled, specifies what commission will be charged, and obliges the author to exclusive representation for the book in question. There should be provisions which spell out how and why the agent-author association may be terminated. It is absolutely unnecessary for an author to agree to any exclusive representation that extends to future work.

Chapter 16

Editing and Publishing Mysteries

An interview with Barbara Peters

Q: *You went into publishing after great success as a bookseller. What motivated this move?*

A: I would never have attempted any form of publishing if my husband, Robert L. Rosenwald, Jr., hadn't been willing to experiment with new forms of technology and with designing yet another new business.

Rob and I originally intended to reprint books we liked that had disappeared. We were intrigued by new technologies for small presses such as Print On Demand. It wasn't long, however, before we discovered that the economics of POD meant at best break-even for a press, and more often a loss, given the costs of editorial (sometimes older books needed either revision, correction, or new introductions and updated bibliographies and biographies), acquisition, typesetting and design, set-up with the POD printer, marketing, and distribution. So we shifted into conventional printing using POD for titles that had either small anticipated sales or titles that we had printed conventionally and then needed to reprint in small quantities after they had paid for themselves. Printing costs all relate to scale; with POD, each unit is unique and thus costs exactly the same as every other unit, so nothing is gained by a raging sales success.

Initially, we wanted to get out-of-print first books in a series back into print plus publish the occasional reference work.

We soon learned that a small press hasn't got the marketing muscle or the distribution to print and sell mass markets, so we rethought our position and elected to move into trade paperbacks with higher price points.

Our next realization was that Big Publishing was focusing more and more on Big Books and ignoring the smaller mystery, which includes the traditional detective story. And as soon as we had some titles in print we started getting query letters from authors asking if we would consider original manuscripts.

In time, original publishing took over our program. We formed an Editorial Review Committee composed of some twenty volunteer readers. We require that all submissions be in electronic format. First the query letter, then, upon invitation, the first thirty pages, which go to members of the ER Committee. Those submissions that survive the first screening go in full manuscript to a second round of readers, and those that survive that process go to me; I make nearly all the final publishing decisions. We are thus well set up to work with unagented authors. An author should ask a press for its submission guidelines, not just fire off a manuscript.

We filled a hole, given the practices of the publishing conglomerates that dominate the industry these days. The success of "small" houses such as ours has spawned a booming small-press industry. Most specialize in a single genre, but some embrace a wide range.

We can define a trade publisher, which is what we are mostly talking about here, as having, at a minimum, these characteristics:

1. Provides editorial services by a professional staff.

2. Does not accept money from authors for publishing their books or engage in copublishing ventures.

3. Has a published discount schedule/terms to the trade.

4. Sells at least 90% of its books as fully returnable or makes its inventory available through a wholesaler or distributor.

5. Has at least two authors on its list, and is not related to a majority of its authors.

6. Provides some kind of marketing/sales services.

Q: *What are book editors and publishers looking for nowadays?*

A: There are several parts to the acquisitions process. It isn't just about what editors like, it's about what sells and how to sell it, plus costs for acquisition, design, production, and marketing. Some books are just too expensive to publish. Some may be too risky, legally or financially. Some may just have to enter an overcrowded field.

Editors get most excited by books they love, but sometimes they are forced to honor contracts made by someone else, or accept a book from an author whose body of work they publish even if they don't care for the current entry, or buy a book to fill a slot. In an ideal world, you fall in love with a book for its voice. It's just like meeting someone at a party and starting a conversation—it's how you react to the person's style and what he has to say.

I have a five-point scale: setting, characterizations, plot, concept or content, and the quality of the writing. Of these, plot is the least important as it's the most easily fixed. You cannot teach writers to be interesting, but you can teach them story structure. Actually, you can't always do that. I've bitten on a few books where I loved the way the author wrote or the concept of the book but could not get a story delivered. Is that the editor's fault or the author's? Hard to say. If the second book proves as difficult to extract as the first, if the author doesn't grow, then no matter how painful, I move on. No writer should assume that selling that first book guarantees a career.

Tips on submission: Master your tools. Spellcheck like mad (and don't confuse *discrete* with *discreet* or fall for other homonyms). Check your grammar (there is a difference between lie and lay, between less and few, between between and among, as well a need for the proper use of pronouns and verb tenses).

Ascertain the house style or use *The Chicago Manual of Style*, and be consistent throughout the book. Do not use the dash as a substitute for proper punctuation. It clutters up the page, and it doesn't suit a lot of books such as historicals. Do not give your characters names that sound alike and thus can be confused. In short, don't waste my time with remedial stuff. Editors are there to read your story, not teach you writing.

But liking a submission isn't the whole story. The pressures are different, depending on what size publishing house you are and who owns you. Big houses, owned by media conglomerates and conscious of capitalization and wide distribution channels, are looking for big sellers, though they still gamble on works they like. Many editors have a mandate from above that forces them to consider books based more on salability than on literary merit. In many cases books have come to equal mass entertainment, and some authors actually admit they are writing for the lowest common denominator to achiece the largest possible sales. Celebrities help drive bestsellers; the star system and agents have come to play dominant roles in New York. Can an author get TV or other media space? Is there a hook for the book?

Everyone wants to publish "what will sell." This can mean tagging on to whatever's "hot"—we've all noticed that a success will spawn any number of imitators and that some news item or social trend will result in a raft of books.

The point is, forget what's selling, what's hot. By the time you can write your book, the world will have changed. Go for your own vision. Be bold. Be creative. It's better to be a leader than a clone.

When I opened The Poisoned Pen bookstore at the end of the 1980s, the received wisdom was that only mysteries by women were selling. Art didn't sell. Series were god. Africa as a setting was death. Books had a certain look which many houses modified from time to time in a process called "refreshing the covers." All of these "truths" have shifted. Series are great for establishing identity, but publishers today: 1. do not want multiple book contracts, two or three being the norm; 2. want more flexibility to sell books to TV/films without giving up a series character; 3. are so impressed with the success of a few major authors writing "standalone" (also called "breakout") books, that it's today's publishing paradigm. Is it a fad or a long-term plan? No one knows.

Series cut two ways. Some can continue to grow their audiences, some level out. A lot depends on the series concept and how well the author succeeds in refreshing it. John Sandford, for instance, has improved the *Prey* series each book and kept it dynamic. Some others (I name no names) either started with an idea that was bound to run out of steam or characters that couldn't grow, or encountered other limiting factors such as the "Cabot's Cove syndrome." Many authors grow restive trying to produce long-running series that can't accommodate plot ideas, restrict location, and feel like a straitjacket.

What are your choices? Write a standalone book. Start a new series. Adopt a pen name. This is a difficult area for publishers of all sizes to deal with. You want your marketing to plant the hook that promises a future book for fans, but you don't want to get locked in. If you are a small press, can you pick up a series that's been dropped and run with it? I've gone both ways, rejecting some, accepting others. There is no absolute rule, especially as you can't always control the backlist when it's published by someone else, which can be crucial to an author's future success.

Small presses tend to focus on books significant to their mission, that are original or well written rather than likely to be bestsellers, and can experiment more with books they like because their overheads are not as punishing. We have made at least one publishing decision based on how much we could afford to lose rather than on how much we expected to make. Luckily, it turned out to earn a modest profit.

A trap we try to avoid is taking on hobby books, books that successful authors like but can't get their ordinary publisher to print. Another publishing pitfall is coming into a series late in the game when the chances of its survival have already been diminished. It's a judgment call, and it's easy to get blinded by your fondness for a work (or an author) to the publisher's overall detriment. Like any business, the first object has to be survival. So small presses do have many of the same constraints as large operations that affect their publishing decisions.

Another factor is what is called "balancing the list." You can't afford to do a raft of similar books lest you get stereotyped and turn away your core audience.

Small publishers do want to concentrate on their genre, whatever it is, but they don't want to get locked into a subgenre unless that is their actual focus. It's important for a successful small publishing plan to have a mission statement that directs its acquisition decisions and helps implement its marketing strategies.

Marketing. There's a topic. If the movies are all about distribution, so is today's publishing. Let's face it: For the most part a small press' marketing strategy is going to be to publish the best books it can and depend upon good reviews and favorable word-of-mouth to get its books noticed, since advertising is prohibitively expensive. It also means its authors have to shoulder a lot of the promotional work. How much energy and money they can expend will make all the difference to how widely their book sells. So a savvy small publisher looks for a creative and committed author, one who, if he or she can't travel to promote, at least has good Internet skills and/or strong personal contacts.

Authors should befriend local booksellers—preferably independents, but use them all. Drop in at libraries wherever you can. Libraries are the bedrock upon which Poisoned Pen Press depends for its initial orders for each new publication. If your book has a very specific focus such as a hobby or a profession or a retail specialty, consider marketing your book in nontraditional outlets such as a kennel club or a needlework shop or an antiques fair.

The savvy author will set up a website, which should contain these basics: a short biography and author photo; a list of all publications sorted by series and in chronological order; any reviews or quotes alongside each title, which can also be made to stand out with a copy of the cover and a brief plot description; and a schedule of appearances and events where the author will be accessible. Buy-my-book buttons should link to the publisher, to booksense.com, or to any independent bookstore that can do mail order. In short, a biography, a bibliography, and an events schedule. You can also capture a mailing list by asking visitors to the website to sign up by email and zip code, and then you can send invitations linked to appearances and mail out periodic announcements or even a regular newsletter.

Luckily there are many tools available to authors at little or no cost, such as email, list-serves like DorothyL, and e-groups (variations of list-serves) like Murder Must Advertise and Independent Mystery Publishers. There are online resources such as ClueLass.com or The Historical Mystery Appreciation Society. Joining the Mystery Writers of America or, if appropriate, the Canadian Crime Writers Association or Britain's Crime Writers Association opens up opportunities and knowledge. Sisters-in-Crime and the Private Eye Writers of America also provide support for authors and collegial exchange. Try those as entry points and follow the tips and suggestions and links they provide.

Individual signings can be organized with some publisher support, but the author should take the initiative to feel out the community and set up events. Regional mystery conferences or Bouchercon, the annual large convention, are a great way to get noticed. Many writers conferences also provide opportunities to get work noticed and rub elbows with fellow writers, agents, and editors.

Q: *What are the advantages and disadvantages of big publishing houses versus small ones? What about online publishing, on-demand publishing, self-publishing?*

A: In big houses, editors read manuscripts and make buying decisions. Copyeditors help prepare the manuscript and verify facts and conform style. There are design teams, art teams, publicity plans, marketing departments, sales departments with catalogues and reps. It's a giant committee. Acquiring editors may find the biggest job they have is selling the book in house, that is, getting the rest of the team behind the book.

A big house has the money to support a project in ways a small press can't, although there is no guarantee that much—if any—promotion will actually be done. This can be affected by the contract, and the author and agent should consider negotiating for promotion as part of any deal. Big houses can offer big advances, freeing some authors to write full-time. Big houses can get the author TV and other media appearances, pay for advertising, send out advanced review copies, set up author tours, pay co-op advertising to retailers. And more.

Small presses can sometimes offer more individualized attention, co-opt the author into marketing, and invite the author into cover design. A savvy small press can sometimes attract more review attention for its authors.

The real distinction, however, is that books that are published by a regular publisher of whatever size go through an editorial process. Several pairs of eyes look at the book. No matter how fine the sieve, how careful the author, error creeps in. Self-editing is risky. The author is not always the best judge of his own work. Also, retailers are more likely to accept "product" that comes through a publishing process rather than through self-publishing or cooperative ventures. Readers have greater confidence in a publishing imprint they recognize.

As a bookseller, I don't have time to screen the masses of co- or self-published material that comes my way. I add books to our inventory and set up events based on reading review copies. All online promotions, referrals to websites, or promotional letters fail with me, since they don't tell me what I want to know: Does the book have an end as good as the beginning? Does it deliver on its promise? Is there too much middle? What about production values?

I am not going to invite my customers to read weak books.

Q: What are the advantages and disadvantages of being published in hardcover as opposed to a paperback original?

A: Hardcover books are more suitable for review. More likely to be considered for review. More likely for library purchase. In mystery, they appeal to the collector market. The higher price point may result in higher earnings and higher royalties, although overall sales really determine the royalties an author receives. There's longevity, too. Hardcovers have longer shelf life. Hardcovers may have more appeal for a larger house for a paperback or other subrights deal.

Q: How much do editors and others in the publishing house deal directly with writers? Or is the agent usually the go-between?

A: In big publishing today, virtually every author who gets a contract is represented by an agent. Very few editors will even read an unagented work, in part because it's a huge timesaver if the agent has done the first screening. The business parts go easier. And it's pleasanter. It's difficult to critique or reject an author's work face to face.

Small presses can and often do review unagented work. I do it all the time since the only opinion that matters to me about publishing a book is my own. I don't have to sell it in-house, either. And while agents can have helped an author shape a book, sometimes they throw up problems if I want to make suggestions or changes. Our contracts are limited to two-book deals and don't demand enormous review. And authors may prefer not to pay 10% or 15% to an agent.

Getting an agent is a decision very much related to the level of publishing the author is targeting. If your sights are set on New York, better find one.

Q: *Please explain all the stuff the publishers do that, from the writer's point of view, happens behind the scenes.*

A: This is a list from Rob, who is the publisher of Poisoned Pen Press:

> Evaluate manuscripts
>
> Select those we are interested in publishing
>
> Negotiate a contract to publish
>
> Get basic book information (author, title, ISBN, binding, price) to Ingram, Baker & Taylor, Bowker, Amazon, and other sales or informational outlets
>
> Edit the manuscript for publication (sometimes called copyediting)
>
> Design the book, have the edited manuscript typeset
>
> Come up with cover concept (in our case, by working with the author, but that is not usual)
>
> Choose an illustrator for the cover or acquire suitable photographs (with permissions)
>
> Get author photo and biography
>
> Send the book out for blurbs
>
> Create jacket copy and promo materials including sell-sheet and press release
>
> Update Ingram, Baker & Taylor, Bowker, Amazon, etc. with cover art, cover copy, author bio, etc.
>
> Get printing quotes and do pricing
>
> Create ARCs, send one to author to proofread
>
> Send out ARC and press release to pre-pub reviewers,

sales reps, and a few select booksellers

Send out ARC to a few select readers who hopefully will begin to get a buzz going on the Internet and elsewhere

Send out sell-sheets and press release to bookstores and to sales reps, prepare seasonal catalogues and other sales tools

Get author's proofed ARC to final proofreader/copy editor

Get corrections typeset

Create final dust jacket

Decide upon print quantity

Send off final typeset book and dust jacket to printer

When finished books come in, send copies to newspaper and magazine reviewers and submit books for awards where appropriate

Check on production schedules and be sure the distributor is stocked

Make sure bookstores that have signings planned have books

Manage sales, shipping, billings (in-house or via a distributor), track royalties

Work with subrights agent(s) to sell audio rights, foreign rights, large print rights, paperback rights, book clubs, film options, and so forth, and track revenues from same

Per contract, pay author for the work less the amount of any advance paid upon signing and/or publication

◇◇◇

This is obviously a monumental task for an author to undertake by himself. It's difficult to flog your own work and overcome credibility issues; sales reps do it better. Also, if the author is busy running the business, when will he create new work? This is another argument for publishing with a press rather than self-publishing.

Chapter 17

The Bookselling Business

An Interview with Otto Penzler

Q: *How do booksellers decide which "first" books to stock on their shelves?*

A: My store, the Mysterious Bookstore in New York City, is a specialty store, and so the things we do are very different from what other, non-specialty stores do. We carry *every* first mystery. Why we carry large quantities of some books and not others is a more pertinent question.

First, early reviews make some difference. *Publisher's Weekly*, especially, as we do not subscribe to *Kirkus* or *Library Journal* or *Booklist* (larger stores might).

Second, the recommendation of sales reps means something IF we know and trust the rep. Steer us wrong because you overpaid for a book and we won't trust you the next time.

Third, if we got galleys (and I've been here long enough that we get virtually every galley) *and* someone at the store actually had time to read it *and* liked it a lot...then we'd heavy up. Probably most important, however, is if the author is available to sign books. In the era of Amazon.com, and with a Barnes & Noble and Borders on every corner, we can no longer sell unsigned books. Well, of course we can, but you know what I mean. If a first-time writer doesn't sign, we might sell a half-dozen of a book we like. If he/she does sign, we might sell 20 to 30 copies, or more.

Q: *What do booksellers do to sell books besides stocking them on their shelves and waiting for customers to come in?*

A: Signing, signing, signing. We want writers to sign their books for us. We don't have formal signings (when writers are present in the store to meet customers and write personal messages for them in the books they buy) anymore, as New Yorkers are just too blasé to show up, or if they do, they bring shopping bags full of remainders for an author to sign, which doesn't do us a lot of good. Other bookstores, of course, believe in formal signings and hold them all the time.

Like many booksellers, we have a monthly newsletter. Ours runs about 40 pages and goes out to a mailing list of many thousands of customers. Names are automatically added when people buy books and automatically dropped if we don't hear from them again for six months. We also have a website which sells some (but not too many) books. We have had several book clubs for many years, in which members automatically receive an autographed first edition every month. The Main Club has the biggest names in the business: Parker, Grafton, Francis, Lehane, Connelly, Patterson, Leonard, Evanovich, Crais, etc. The Hard-Boiled Club speaks for itself, as does the Soft-Boiled Club and the First Mystery Club. We also have a British Club, in which members receive an autographed first edition of a British book by a British writer (P.D. James, Minette Walters, Reginald Hill, etc.). And an Unclassifiable Club for literary mysteries (Joyce Carol Oates, Umberto Eco, Alan Furst) and books that don't fall into any real category (Donald Westlake, maybe).

Writers can help their own cause by showing up to sign when they say they're going to. Since the publishers' publicity departments set up the signings and are generally not as competent as one might wish, mainly because they're overworked, any enterprising and/or ambitious writer should get out the yellow pages, call every bookstore in town, and ask if he can come by to sign. Some advance notice means the store has the chance to order more books before the author arrives with pen in hand.

Q: *What should authors know about the differences between specialty stores such as yours, and general-interest bookstores, chains, and online sellers?*

A. There are lots of differences. This could be a book by itself. Or a big chapter, at least.

Specialty stores actually care about the authors and their customers. So do most general bookstores, if they are independents. The chains will not know who you are unless you're named Grisham or Clancy. The price clubs (which mainly sell books by the top 20 sellers—and sell them by the truckload, by the way) don't know what a book is. Any author who worries about price clubs is either dreaming, because his book won't be there, or is greedy because he's miffed that the clubs sold only 150,000 copies his last novel and he'd hoped for 200,000. As for online booksellers who don't also have a bricks-and-mortar outlet, Amazon leads the world, of course, and it sells lots of books based on convenience and some discount, though most of those heavy discounts disappeared just about when most independent stores went out of business, same as at the chains.

The collector market is a fairly good-sized one in the mystery field, and I know of no intelligent collector who buys online, and not too many who will ever have a good collection who buy from the chains. The independents, especially specialty stores, know something about first editions and how to sell them. They care about condition if they're shipping, and they work hard to get books signed for their collectors. I would say, for example, that in my store fully 50 percent of the hardcover books I sell go to collectors.

Q: *How can first-time/unestablished authors work with booksellers?*

A: Booksellers appreciate drop-ins but mainly if an author calls first (or a representative from his publisher does). The author needs to take a lot of responsibility, however. It is common for us to arrange signings with authors, buy 30 or 50 books, then wait around for an author who never shows up. We hate that author until, two years later, we meet him and he swears no one at his publishing house told him about the signing. I believe the author 90 percent of the time.

Sending publicity stuff to bookstores, whether it's email, letters, postcards, mugs, T-shirts, bookmarks, posters, etc., is pretty much a waste of time and money. Booksellers aren't idiotic enough to think they're getting something exclusive.

A personal phone call saying, "I'll be in New York next month. Would you like me to drop in to sign whatever books you have?" is, for me, the single best thing an author can do. And, when you get there, be a pro like Mary Higgins Clark or Sue Grafton or Mike Connelly and pretend you're enjoying the experience. Take the time to get to know the booksellers' names. I know authors who make notes after leaving so they can greet the bookseller by name on the next visit. This is smart. Booksellers don't get into this field to get rich. They like books and authors, and they are excited to meet authors and flattered when they are remembered. It's hard, but it's worth it

I've always been a huge believer in the ripple effect. You may sell only ten books at a signing, but if everyone loves you, they'll tell their friends, and sellers will tell other customers. This has worked to the great advantage of Larry Block and James Ellroy, among others, who tirelessly promoted their books at bookstores, took the time to chat with the clerks and the owners, and went back book after book until they became so well known and liked that when a customer asked, "What should I read?" the first name that came to the bookseller's mind was that particular author's.

Q: *So why did you decide to open a mystery bookstore?*

A: Every bookseller I know loves books. That's why we went into the bookselling business. Ironically, we all read more before we opened our stores. We had more time then. None of us imagined how many hours of a day it took to make the business work.

Sure, we knew it wasn't all sitting around reading books and then discussing them with customers (which is what most customers believe—"You know, when I retire I think I'll open a bookstore" is my favorite), but you're still never ready for it. Store hours are the easy part. It's restocking shelves, dealing with paperwork, and mainly trying to figure out how to pay the bills, get off credit hold, pay the staff and the insurance and the medical insurance and the phone bills and utilities and taxes and supplies and rent and trash pickup and the Internet provider and, oh yes, is there anything left for me? Well, maybe next week.

Another thing booksellers appreciate is when authors actually support their local bookstore. Every mystery writer who shows up here talks about all the books he's read, and I note that none of them is ever bought from me. Linda Fairstein and Mike Connelly are two exceptions. There might be others over the past 24 years, but I can't think of any. I don't expect it from out-of-towners, but I remain stunned that it never occurs to all the New York writers that the guy who supports them so strongly never seems worthy of reciprocal support.

Bookselling is the greatest business I know. I suppose I do a lot of whining, but I wouldn't trade it for anything. Most customers are great, and most authors are, too, especially in the mystery field. There are the always a few jerks, but most writers are fun to be around. And there are always plenty of books. Sometimes it's hard to remember the days when I had to choose between having lunch or buying a book, and it's easy now to take for granted that books are everywhere around me, but I sometimes lean back and take it all in and realize how blessed I am. No kidding.

Chapter 18

Catch-23: Publicizing Your Mystery Novel

Jeremiah Healy

Congratulations! You've figured out how to beat the first-time-novelist's Catch-22 ("I can't get published without a literary agent but I can't get a literary agent without being published") and your mystery novel has been accepted by a publisher.

Sorry. There's a Catch-23, too: "I thought my job as author was done," but, "My job as marketeer has just begun."

Why?

The publishing industry has changed tremendously since I broke into it twenty years ago. I've been lucky enough to have had thirteen books published in the John Francis Cuddy private-eye series, two standalone suspense novels, three (and counting) books in the Mairead O'Clare legal-thriller series, and three collections of my short stories. However, if I were starting out today, my prognosis might not be so bright.

Again, why?

When I served on the Edgar Award committee for best first novel in 1987, we received 21 submissions. When I chaired the same committee in 1998, we received 117 submissions. That's over FIVE TIMES more than just eleven years earlier.

What's happening?

It's simple economics: In the two decades since 1984, the number of New York independent publishing houses has shrunk from 34 to 6. That's right. Six. Bertelsman, the Germany-based media conglomerate, alone owns all the imprints of Random House, Doubleday, Delacorte, Dell, and Bantam. To finance the acquisition of all these subsidiary imprints, tremendous pressure has been put on their editors to find the next Patricia Cornwell or John Grisham. The good news is that more first novels are getting published at most imprints. The bad news is that generally right-out-of-college, overworked and underpaid staff publicists at those imprints are being asked to push too many new authors, or are being told to focus on only a few new authors.

Unless you are one of the chosen few, you lose on both counts.

Until you're famous, you've got to be your own publicist.

I'm going to suggest a number of ways. Some are unconventional. None guarantees success. So feel free to accept some, and to reject others, depending on what makes the most sense to you.

Use a pseudonym

If your publisher hasn't yet listed you in its catalog or commissioned the book jacket, consider using a pseudonym.

Why?

If your actual first or last name is difficult to pronounce, people might feel uncomfortable asking for your novel in a bookstore. If your last name falls near the end of the alphabet, market studies show that many customers never reach your shelf. Most browsers begin at the earliest part of the mystery section they can see easily at their eye-level. Browsers have only so much money and only so much hand span to hold only so many books (I've never understood why more bookstores don't have carts or those hang-from-the-forearm baskets like gourmet grocery and office supply stores). There are, of course, exceptions to this alphabetical barrier: Well-known mystery authors such as William G. Tapply, Donald Westlake, and R. D. Zimmerman have done just fine selling their books from the wrong end of the alphabet. But playing the percentages helps.

For example, while I've written the Cuddy novels and short story collections under my own name, I decided to use the pseudonym "Terry Devane" for the Mairead O'Clare legal thrillers because "D" names are not just near the beginning of the alphabet; they're also generally stacked within a foot of eye level for most browsers.

Invest your advance

Chances are you will receive only a small advance for a first mystery, somewhere around $1,000 from the smaller imprints, maybe as much as $10,000 from the larger. I'm not scoffing at these sums, but your agent takes 15 percent off the top, and Uncle Sam gets another 25 percent. Your share won't substantially improve your standard of living.

I recommend investing what's left in publicity. Now that you're a published author, you can file a Schedule C with your 1040, and deduct these outlays as business expenses.

What are the best ways to invest your advance?

Join the writers organizations such as Private Eye Writers of America, Mystery Writers of America, Sisters-in-Crime (yes, they welcome male members), and the International Association of Crime Writers. All will provide you with newsletters and the opportunity to attend regional/state chapter meetings to network with other authors. The calendar sections of the newsletters will help you locate marketing and publicity resources.

Focus globally

Your publisher's staff publicist is overworked and underpaid and is unlikely to give you the resources and attention you want. The solution: hire your own publicist. Publicists, for a fee, compose professional press releases and send them electronically around the country—indeed, the world—to the many forums in their databases that you'd spend more time compiling on your own than you did writing that novel. Independent publicists also can help you create the hook that might make your novel newsworthy and persuade some forums to run an article on it or on you.

Usually this hook has to be something nonfiction about your fictional mystery novel. For example, my sixth Cuddy novel, *Right to Die*, deals with a fictional law professor who crusades for the right to assisted suicide, only to receive anonymous and ominous death threats. It appeared the same summer that Dr. Jack Kevorkian was indicted for "helping" others to the other side. That nonfiction tie-in was the hook that landed me national interviews, talk-show appearances, etc.

You need to be in publicity for the long haul, but your hook needn't be so dramatic. For example, if your novel deals with an amateur sleuth who's into quilting as a hobby, a good publicist will trigger interviews and articles in some of the quilting magazines. Don't laugh. I'm told there are about twenty such publications that are read rabidly by just the self-selecting audience of fans you'd love to reach with your quilting-murder novel.

You should have a website. Visit mine at www.jeremiahhealy.com or Bill Tapply's at www.williamgtapply.com for ideas. A website is a great service to readers, reviewers, and booksellers—precisely the people who are crucial to your success.

Ask a friend with a good digital camera to take some color and black-and-white head shots of you. Once the friend provides you with some high-quality emailed photos, you can print out facsimiles as needed for magazines, newspapers, etc., since a professional-looking photo greatly enhances your chances of a distant forum running a text piece about your novel. Just be sure your friend gets a photo credit when the head shot is used, and that you send him or her a copy of the tearsheet from the publication.

Focus regionally

Okay, let's be realistic: Unless your novel contains some especially compelling hook, *Time* or *USA Today* is not likely to be speed-dialing you for an interview. However, if your city, region, or state has a magazine, they might love to publish an article about a native son or daughter. Ditto alumni, business, and professional magazines that do short pieces on the theme: "Did you know that X writes mysteries, too?"

If you join Sisters-in-Crime, for example, you can obtain a list of mailing labels for bookstores. If you cannot justify hiring an independent publicist, plaster the stores with some kind of press kit (information about the book, a bio of you, and that photo) about you and your book. Drive to these stores and introduce yourself to the manager, always leaving enough copies of the kit for all employees, so they feel you have reached out and touched them, too.

Don't bother scheduling formal signings in distant bookstores for your first book. Readers tend not to show up to meet an author they've never heard of, and you and the bookstore staff will stand around, excruciatingly embarrassed, for one of the longest hours of your life, making awkward small talk.

The place for your first formal signing is your neighborhood bookstore.

Finally, the calendar sections of those authors organizations' newsletters list regional fan conventions, writers conferences, and—for the most bang for the buck—regional conferences of the American Booksellers Association, such as the New England Booksellers Association and the Southeast Booksellers Association. Even if your publisher won't have a table at such events, one of the organizations you belong to might. Volunteer to staff it for a few hours so you can meet and hand a copy of your press kit to the attending bookstore owners and managers from your region in a very time-and-cost-efficient way.

Focus locally

The former Speaker of the House, Tip O'Neill, once said, "All politics is local." First-time authors can substitute "publicity" for "politics," because you must build a solid local fan base to be successful. And it's generally free, or close to it.

First, hit your local newspapers. Typically they are dying to run feature articles on area folks, and they can time the appearance of the story to coincide with your big, local bookstore signing to which you will invite every human being who possibly might attend.

Second, many local high schools and libraries have speaker programs. Seek them out. Never turn down an invitation. It's a great way for you to become comfortable at public presentation, and there are several hidden advantages. Often high school librarians will attend a class day and then recommend you to their librarian friends at other schools. Also, a librarian from Town A might "audition" you by being in the audience at your library talk in Town B, and if you do well, she may invite you to speak at her venue.

Schools and libraries often receive grants for paying speakers honoraria. I've received as little as $25 for gas and tolls, and as much as $2,000 for a one-hour speech. Don't be afraid to ask about honoraria: They enable you to earn back some of that advance that you've spent on other publicity.

Third, approach your local cable-access television station. These outlets are required by law to provide "cultural" content during their broadcast hours, and you, a published author, qualify. The best of these shows are interview situations, with two chairs, a coffee table displaying your book, and an interviewer who knows how to ask questions. He or she typically will urge you to huck your novel shamelessly, creating, in effect, a free infomercial all about you.

It gets better: Station A in your town produces the show, then repeats the broadcast ten or twelve times during the next few weeks at various times of day and night on its channel, thus reaching a self-selecting audience of book-lovers that no direct-mail expert could target.

Even better, Station A will license that half-hour show to Stations B through Z in other towns, since it's cheaper for those stations to pay a usage fee to A than to produce independent shows themselves. And then they broadcast your show to their self-selecting book-loving audiences. For a few hours of your time, you get incredible impact and breadth.

One important point: Even if you have to buy them yourself (at your author's discount), bring enough copies of your book to inscribe not only for the interviewer, but also for the camera operators, the director, and everyone else who helps produce the show. It's a matter of courtesy and gratitude, and it's likely to get you invited back when your next novel comes out.

Closing comments

Regardless of what kind of publicity you do, be yourself. Don't try to imitate anybody. People like, trust, and appreciate sincerity; they suspect phonies.

If you take your job as self-publicist seriously and do it effectively, your book will sell well enough that when your next one comes out, your publisher will have its publicity and marketing departments handle the work for you.

Chapter 19

Persistence

Vicki Stiefel

Two men stand on beach, the surf tickling their feet. Charlie yells, "Hey, Phil. I got a great title for my next novel!"

Phil smiles. "And it is?"

"*Bleaching the Bones*." Charlie slaps his thigh. "Isn't that great?"

"Wow," says Phil. He moves a little to the right and casts his lure into the sea. He's shaking his head. He happens to know that Charlie, who calls himself a novelist, has never written a word in his life. But he's come up with lots of terrific titles for novels.

〈〉〈〉〈〉

Persistence is about the start—actually putting the pen to page, the fingers to keyboard. If you don't start, you'll never get there.

〈〉〈〉〈〉

What does it take to persist until your novel is published? Guts, insanity, intensity, determination, stubbornness, and, most of all, passion.

〈〉〈〉〈〉

For me, novel writing is creative and exciting. It's all about feelings. It's also, emphatically, about getting published. Writing with any other goal is like one hand clapping. Very Zen, but not where I'm at.

I write for many reasons. Writing satisfies something deep and personal inside me. But I always aim to get published.

<><><>

Maybe it's all about our individual need to overcome obstacles. Maybe persistence in writing a novel is simply a desperate, stubborn belief that it *matters*.

Writing, and the persistence it takes to do it—to finish, revise, rewrite, edit, and sell a story or a novel—fulfills my need to have my imagination transformed into reality.

<><><>

Phil the surf-caster knows all about persistence.

He was always a doer, a worker, a mover. An Olympic-caliber fencer in college, he knew what it meant to dig in, to work hard, and to keep going when the going got tough. Phil had grit, and he usually succeeded. After college, he attended the esteemed Iowa Writer's Workshop. Then, bam! He sold his first novel. Not bad, eh?

Another novel soon flowed from his pen. It went…nowhere. Rejection notes filled his files.

Years passed. Phil got married, taught college English, sired children, traveled. And he continued to write novels—seven or eight of them, he can't quite remember. He completed a novel every year or two. He kept writing novels.

He got nothing but rejections. After that first triumph, Phil met with no success at all.

But he persisted.

Twenty years after the sale of his first novel, he sold his second one.

Philip R. Craig now writes the popular Martha's Vineyard mystery series.

<><><>

Don't give up. It's simple. Those three words define persistence

But, really, it's all a crock, right? Surely, you're thinking, I wouldn't have been asked to write this chapter in this book unless I'd published a novel. So who am I to talk?

What about all the hopeful writers who persist...and never make it, never get published, get nothing but rejections? No one asks them to write chapters about persistence.

Persistence alone matters.

It's not a crock.

<>‹›‹›

Here's the recipe. True, it doesn't work for everyone. You can follow the recipe and still fail. Haven't you ever made a lousy meal even though you followed the recipe?

But if you *don't* follow this recipe, you stand *no chance* of getting published.

Write every day.

Read all sorts of fiction. Read constantly.

Join a workshop or writing group.

Complete your manuscript. Finish what you start.

Revise it. Then revise it some more.

Give it to several trusted readers. Ask for their suggestions. Insist on candor.

Revise it again.

Get an agent.

Keep doing it.

Keep learning, improving, applying what you learn.

‹›‹›‹›

In 1993, I joined a writers group. We had a dozen members, and each week we read two of our members' pieces. Most readings were from novels-in-progress.

One member, Ethan, was a talented writer. His stories were rich in voice and personality. He could paint vivid scenes and create memorable characters. But he was still a novice. Even his best stuff needed revising.

Whenever Ethan's work was critiqued, he'd take copious notes and listen intently to our discussion about the scenes he'd presented to the group. We'd comment on what he'd written with great thought and energy and feeling, all with the aim of helping him make it better.

A few weeks later when Ethan's turn came around again, our group would listen to the beginning of yet another new novel.

Ethan refused to revise. Whenever one of his scenes was critiqued and suggestions were offered, he gave up on it and started a new story, thinking maybe this time he'd get it right.

Rather than persist in honing what he'd written, much of which was wonderful, he abandoned it.

Ethan never did get anything published. Last I heard, he had quit writing. Such a waste of talent.

Finish the last word on the last page. Then dig in. Revise and edit. Hone those words, make those cuts, discard that character, shift that scene.

Writing a first draft is a monumental accomplishment. Editing it until it sings is even bigger.

⟨⟩⟨⟩⟨⟩

You're going to get rejected. And rejected again. And again. By agents. By editors. By publishers.

Remember: It's not YOU that's being rejected. It's your work.

⟨⟩⟨⟩⟨⟩

Nowadays you need an agent to sell your novel. You must submit your chapters to countless agents. They have the privilege of being your first rejectors.

So now you've got stacks of agent rejections. You must stink. It's time to quit. What's the point? Why bother? It's too much work, heartbreak, and frustration.

A lot of people quit. What we know for certain about quitters is: They will never be published.

So persist.

Have faith in yourself and your work. Go back to it and sweat and write and edit some more.

Stick to the recipe.

And, finally, maybe you'll get a nibble from an agent. Then a bite.

<><><>

Persistence is just *doing it*. Not thinking about doing it or worrying about doing it. Doing it.

Keep writing.

Keep improving.

Keep getting feedback.

Keep submitting.

Submit only your very best work. Agents and editors don't want to see half-baked or half-finished material. They're not interested in potential. They want something to publish.

<><><>

I meet Susie Editor at a writers conference. She loves my pitch, so at her request, I send her three chapters and a synopsis.

> Phone call: Hi, Vicki, this is Suzie Editor. I *love* it! The characters are great. The plot's terrific. Please send the complete manuscript.

I'm thrilled. I send it.

> Phone call: Hi, Vicki, this is Suzie Editor again. Wow! I love your book. We want to buy it, but I'd like you to make a few changes first.

She has a long list of suggested changes. Most of them make good sense to me.

I make them all and send them to Suzie.

Two months pass. No word from Suzie Editor. I call her and get her voice mail. I leave a message.

Another two weeks go by. I call again.

Molly Editor answers. I'm afraid, she says, Susie's no longer with us. I'd be happy to look at your manuscript? Send me three chapters.

But wait. Susie has the whole novel. She said you guys wanted to buy it.

Sorry, Molly says. Never heard of it. Just send the chapters and a synopsis, please.

So I send Molly Editor the revised three chapters and a synopsis.

She doesn't like my heroine. Nor does she like the plot. Or the setting. In fact, there's nothing she does like about my novel.

Sorry, says Molly Editor. No sale.

I'm depressed for a week.

Then I pull out the recipe. And I write, write, write.

‹›‹›‹›

Why bother?

All writers at one time or another have asked themselves: Why bother? Everyone experiences that frustration. I sure have. Four unpublished novels hide under my bed. At one point, after asking myself Why Bother for the millionth time, I took up gardening. Others writers I know have taken up sushi making, scuba diving, needlepoint. Most passions are less stressful than writing.

Many writers get discouraged and quit. That's the end of any possible career.

Everyone who's been published has gone back to writing.

If you return to writing, you stand a chance of getting published. If you don't, you have no chance at all.

‹›‹›‹›

If it's in you, you will, and if it's not, you won't. But be aware that others have walked this same path you're walking now. Most successful writers faced a lot of early rejection and discouragement. They persisted.

Persistence isn't all about fighting battles. There will also be admiration for your doggedness, for the fact that you've actually finished a novel. Others will care that you're writing, and they'll pull for you.

You should take pride in persisting. Persistence is admirable.

If you persist, you will reward not only yourself, but also your friends and your loved ones, when, finally, you see your book in print.

It feels swell. I know.

After twelve years of writing novels, of submitting manuscripts, of opening rejection letters, of landing an agent, of getting more rejections...I finally received an enthusiastic acceptance from a publisher.

My first novel is in print. Twelve years....

Now I've gone back to the recipe. I'm writing a new novel, and I know I'll have to persist all over again.

Believe, me, the second time is easier.

To receive a free catalog of Poisoned Pen Press titles, please contact us in one of the following ways:

Phone: 1-800-421-3976
Facsimile: 1-480-949-1707

Email: info@poisonedpenpress.com
Website: www.poisonedpenpress.com

Poisoned Pen Press
6962 E. First Ave. Ste 103
Scottsdale, AZ 85251

Printed in the United States
76582LV00001B/157-192